THE

STORIES AND REFLECTIONS

RULES

ON UNLEARNING

WE

PATRIARCHAL MASCULINITY

LIVE BY

DESTYN A'DANTE LAND

Scriptures marked KJV are taken from the King James Version, public domain.

Scriptures marked ASV are taken from the American Standard Version, public domain.

Cover design by Vanessa Mendozzi

Interior design and formatting by KUHN Design Group | kuhndesigngroup.com

Back cover illustration by Joiterius Marshall

Editing by Kimberley Lim

To the boys and men who have felt like they don't quite fit,
who have struggled to find their place in the world, and who
are now on the journey of self-discovery and acceptance.

To myself and to the child who did weird things,
who laughed and cried, danced and played.

We are, and will always be, special and beautiful, just as we are.

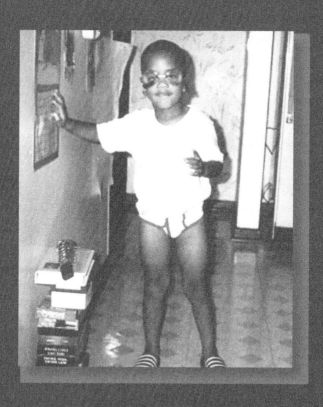

CONTENTS

Foreword 7

Introduction: It Just Doesn't Look Right! 11

I. Shame 25

II. Image 39

III. Anger 51

IV. Gentleness 65

V. Silence 77

VI. Accountability 89

VII. Brotherhood 107

VIII. Fatherhood 121

IX. Love 133

X. Wholeness 153

Epilogue 171

Acknowledgments 177

Author's Bio 179

FOREWORD

In *The Rules We Live By*, we are invited by Destyn not only to sit with the systems, but more importantly to sit with the people—the people who have been deemed as disposable because they were not "man enough," or because they desired to destroy the box and wished to go against the grain of societal norms known as the rules we live by. This text is a call to uncover the truth attached to one's tears, unexplainable anger, and loneliness at the hands of alienation due to not fitting inside the box.

Further, one is encouraged to lead with an ethic of care for the work of deconstruction that is required to fully release oneself from the prison, the box, the closet known as patriarchal masculinity and "what is not right" as it pertains to gender performance. This never-ending thought or feeling of "what is not right" should move one to think through the ways that the prison tells us which colors, toys, songs, clothing, extracurricular activities like sports and dancing, and classes like home economics and woodshop should only be associated with a specific gender. This book nudges us to interrogate our discomfort with "what is not right." The reader is provided a space to reflect on their own harm and how they may have harmed others due to the rules we live by.

I believe this text speaks to the loophole in the rules that many have been searching for, the attempt to make room for "both." I name both as the room for a boy to wear blue and still aspire to be a ballet dancer, the room for a girl to play with an Easy-Bake Oven and still desire to be a carpenter, or the room for none of these things to even matter—simply the loophole to exist. Throw all of the rules away. When the rules are gone, there is a liberty to lean into the curiosity of what would occur if the rules were not governing society. This liberty looks like boys not having to sneak and play with their sisters' dolls or girls not being scrutinized for wanting to rough play with the boys. Sitting with the titles of each chapter, one should come to terms with understanding how the social constructions of gender and masculinity are the gateway to anxiety, fear, depression, and insecurity. The desire to escape the rigid discomfort of not fitting into the box makes one uneasy and afraid. Children and adults have to endure a mental rollercoaster as they strategize ways to live outside of the box in a safe way, which society often doesn't make space for. But the good news is that it starts with us.

The journey to becoming our whole selves, our healed selves, is lifelong. On this journey, we see a young Destyn staring embarrassment, anger, and body dysmorphia in the face. Unfortunately, Destyn's default was to prove his masculinity as he desired, like many of us, to live up to the standard of manhood. This standard was made known at home, in church, in school, and in the media—it was nearly inescapable for Destyn—but he persisted through the journey. This body of work holds space for mistakes made on the journey. It holds space for one to grieve through their journey. Most importantly, the text is grounded in a spirit of endurance and tenacity. I know these descriptors hold tension for marginalized communities. With this work, the reader is encouraged to honor the mistakes, navigate the grief, and keep going, which is what Destyn did to discover his whole self. We are invited to do the same. We are invited to weather the storm as it is a significant part of becoming and being free.

If you're looking for a text that absolves you of your wrongs, this is not it. This is a text that will give us tools to name, recognize, and understand how societal wickedness has hindered our journey to being free. *The Rules We Live By* explicitly addresses how men and women can tear down these ideologies that "make boys into men" through activities like Boy Scouts, city league football, or rites of passage that are embedded within cultures across the world. This is a text that will serve as a roadmap or a GPS for us to no longer carelessly assign unvoiced expectations to girls and women—marriage timeline, duties of a wife, childbirth minimum, and appropriate hairstyles. All of the aforementioned contribute to continuing a cycle of producing broken, confused, and confined human beings. Destyn suggests that we discontinue the cycle by asking the hard questions: Why do I feel like I am not "man enough"? How have I perpetuated the monstrosity that is patriarchy? When did I learn that being angry was okay? Beyond asking these questions, the reader is also welcome to expand their journey through devotionals. However, it is important not to confuse the text with "another Christian book" because that is not what this is. This is an opportunity to consider what spiritual implications exist as we untangle what we thought was "right."

Thank you, Destyn, for penning what I believe will be the catalyst for the freedom and self-discovery of many. This book is "right" in the sense that it sees boys, men, and even girls and women. *The Rules We Live By* holds the pieces of our life together and contributes to our recovery as we learn to love ourselves, accept ourselves, and not only free ourselves but also free others. May we break all the rules, rip up all of the boxes, and liberate ourselves from societal expectations that we were never created to meet.

Terrance McQueen, MDiv
Yale Divinity School
Reverend Frederick J. Streets Social Justice Prize Recipient
John W. Cook Prize in Religion and the Arts Recipient

IT JUST DOESN'T LOOK RIGHT!

Years ago, when my niece Khamani was twelve years old, she sat at the kitchen table of my parents' home and asked me to guess what instrument she played in school. I pretended to pause and think for a few seconds, and quickly guessed either the flute or clarinet. (As a former band geek, I just want to say I have always disliked the clarinet and flute sections. The strongest sections were always the brass and the saxophones.)

She then asked me a question out of the blue that surprised me. "Uncle Destyn, do you think there are some instruments that are just for girls?" *Shoot*, I thought to myself. Was my niece about to call me out for the way I had reinforced my own gender expectations onto her by my assumption that she played the flute or clarinet?

"No, it's just an instrument. Anyone can play whichever one they choose," I responded. She gave me 'the face,' and if you know my niece, you know exactly what face it was. Her eyes met mine with

11

skepticism, and she paused and pondered. "I don't know... I saw a boy walking with a flute... and uh... it just didn't look right."

I sat with those five words that my niece had said—"it just didn't look right"—and kept playing them over and over in my head. These words triggered a series of memories during my adolescence of hearing things like, "You can't do, be, say, walk, or act like that—because it just doesn't look right."

The question my niece asked me is one that I believe we should all ask ourselves at some point in our lives—what's for boys, and what's for girls?

From the moment our mothers find out our sex in the womb, a story is created about who we are and who we will be. If the sex is male, we will adorn the baby in blue—even though before boys wore blue, they wore pink, a softer color of red symbolizing strength and power.[1] (As red became more associated with love and romanticism, pink was rebranded for girls, suggesting that females are closer to emotions like love compared to males.) And as he grows up, we will assume that he will transition from plush animal dolls to wanting to play with trucks, action figures, and toy guns—all because he's a boy.

As a child, I loved my WWE action figures and enjoyed making them fight and wrestle. However, I also yearned to discover how to operate my older sister's old Easy-Bake Oven. Sneaking into the basement, I would search for its bright pink-and-purple box, dust it off, plug it in, and try to replicate the magic I had seen in commercials. A toy that could bake real cookies, brownies, and even cakes seemed like the coolest thing imaginable. Still, I knew I couldn't have this

---

1. Maleigha Michael, "Sexism in Colors—Why Is Pink for Girls and Blue for Boys? - UMKC Women's Center," UMKC Women's Center - Advancing gender equity, June 25, 2018, https://info.umkc.edu/womenc/2018/06/25/8369/.

particular toy, or experience its kind of magic. Similar to my niece's thoughts, I believed "it just didn't look right."

I've spent a large chunk of my life living with a heightened awareness of what does and doesn't look right for boys. This awareness often led me to decide to give up interests, activities, and maybe even key parts of my identity based on my desire to be considered a "real man." In this book, I want to take you on a journey of my transition from boyhood to manhood. Along this journey, you will find stories of me trying to fit into boxes that were never designed for me. And these stories all have origins in the place where I grew up.

I was born and raised in Rondo, a historically Black neighborhood in Saint Paul, Minnesota. The important thing to note about this neighborhood is that you will never find another one like it in Minnesota, and perhaps not even in the Midwest. It's a neighborhood that has a little bit of everything. To paint a picture, across the street lived a Black man who was a medical doctor—the same doctor who delivered me in the hospital. Across from him was a Black painter and artist whose work was displayed throughout the city, even in our own home. The list could go on and on. Black residents on my block were business owners and pastors. Even our city's first Black mayor had a home on our block.

This experience on the block also coexisted with others that might clash in most brains. At the end of the block, you would find the infamous liquor store where teenage boys sold drugs on the street outside. It wasn't abnormal for us to see people intoxicated in the morning or to encounter individuals passed out at the neighborhood park or bus stop—this, too, was part of our community. There wasn't a clear separation between those two realities.

As I got older, I realized that there were unwritten rules for navigating my neighborhood, as well as the rules that governed the schools I attended (which consisted predominantly of students of color, with large populations of Black, Southeast Asian, and White students). These rules dictated how I should act, look, and behave. They were not passed on through a rule book but were taught to us by our older brothers or the older boys at school.

If these rules were to be written down, they might look something like this:

> **Rule #1:** Every man must know how to fight—and if any man disrespects you, you have to fight him to show that you're not a *punk*.

This rule relates to the second one:

> **Rule #2:** Don't act or look like a *bitch*. Once you're labeled as such, people will target you more; in other words, don't show fear, even if you are afraid.

> **Rule #3:** Stay out of the way. Learn not to stare at people for too long, avoid drawing too much attention to yourself, and refrain from asking too many questions.

It was these rules that first introduced me to feelings of anxiety, but the older boys always implied that these rules were teaching me how to be a man.

Although I may not have had the language to describe it at the time, looking back, I've realized that becoming a man is every boy's greatest pursuit. Each lesson boys learn and every decision they make is about attaining this title.

I desperately wanted to become a man, so I tried to follow the unwritten rules that society imposed on me based on my gender. These rules became more complicated as I grew older, and eventually, I understood that they may vary depending on the situation. The rules for Black boys certainly weren't the same as those for White boys.

College was the place where I first began asking questions about masculinity. I knew that I always felt like I had to follow all these rules to fit in or to survive, but I didn't directly connect them to masculinity until coming across the TED Talk "A Call to Men," by Tony Porter.[2] In his talk, Porter describes the "Man Box," which pressures men to embody strength, success, power, dominance, fearlessness, control, and emotional suppression. In the "Man Box," women are perceived as objects, owned by men, and deemed to be of lower worth compared to men.

The "Man Box" gave me language to describe everything that I had been thinking and feeling about masculinity. It truly was a rigid, one-size-fits-all box that I didn't fit into. At the end of his talk, Porter tells a story about a conversation he had with a nine-year-old boy. In this conversation, he asked him: "What would life be like for you if you didn't have to adhere to this Man Box?"

The boy responded, "I would be free."

The boy's words turned on the lights in me, the lights that the rules had dimmed.

I spent my last year of college in Dr. Jeremy Myers's "Rethinking Youth and Adolescence" course trying to make sense of Black

2. Tony Porter, "A Call to Men," TED Talk, December 2010, https://www.ted.com/talks/tony
_porter_a_call_to_men?language=en.

masculinity and the experiences of Black boys. I finished the course feeling like I had only scratched the surface, and I wanted more. After finishing my bachelor's degree, I enrolled in graduate school to study youth development; more specifically, I wanted to explore how young people's understanding of masculinity or femininity shaped the way they lived their lives and made decisions.

The more I learned about masculinity, the more I saw the way it impacted almost every dimension of our lives. I saw how patriarchal masculinity opens the door for women to be abused as the rules imply that women are to be subjected to men; therefore, their assaults and their bruised bodies were not the fault of men but their own. I saw how the patriarchy attempts to keep women in the shadows, silencing their voices and pushing them into a similar box—the boxes of caretaking, nurturing, and submission. I saw how masculine egos started wars both around the world and in the community. Most importantly, I saw how patriarchal masculinity worked to move our world further away from love.

As extreme as it may sound, I saw that if something didn't change, patriarchal masculinity would kill us all.

Sitting with this reality made me want to get involved, but I wasn't sure how. While scrolling through my Facebook feed in 2021, I saw a viral post calling out men for having podcasts that were all about telling women what to do, among other misogynistic crap. The post went on to say that, instead, there's a need for men to have podcasts that address their own issues and address the harm that men are doing to the world. This post felt like a divine call—shortly after reading it, I started the podcast and Instagram account, *Rethinking Manhood*.

On the podcast, I sought to bring men together to tell their stories of navigating masculinity: their stories of shame, insecurity, trauma, and how they've been able to heal. At first, I didn't really expect too much to come from it. To promote the podcast, I made various posts describing the relationship between patriarchal masculinity and other topics, and some of these posts started to get shared and reposted, reaching more people than I could have ever imagined. Its reach made me see how many men were similar to me—struggling to live in a box that never fit and searching for a way to be free from it.

The book you are reading now is an extension of the podcast and content from *Rethinking Manhood*, but also an extension of my journey.

LET'S GET ON THE SAME PAGE

In my conversations about masculinity with other men, I've learned that it is so important to define what we're talking about. Without grounding our conversation in a shared understanding of terms, we may find ourselves having two drastically different discussions. *Feminism*, *patriarchy*, and *masculinity* are all pivotal words to define before reading this book. I'll admit—these words can certainly be intimidating if you're unfamiliar with them. You may have already formed your own opinions on these concepts, and regardless of how you enter this space, I encourage you to stick with me as I hope to make these words digestible and accessible for all readers.

What tends to scare men about this word, *feminism*,[3] is the presumption that its ideologies exist to tell them who they are and what

---

3. If you are new to engaging with feminist theory or are skeptical about it, remember that you do not need to adopt an all-or-nothing approach. You can agree with some scholars and disagree with others, and still acknowledge the benefits and relevance of feminist theory. It's possible to engage with and learn from feminist thought without feeling obligated to accept every idea or perspective without critique.

they should be. My own initial hesitation to read the work of feminist scholars was based on my belief that feminism consisted of just a group of man-hating women claiming their own superiority to men. But as I engaged in feminist texts, I found that the theory was quite the opposite. At face value, feminism is an ideology (of many strands, eras, and approaches) that aims to establish justice, equity, and liberation for women and people of all genders—including men.

Feminism is truly something that benefits everyone. It was feminist politics that advocated for male victims of sexual assault, pushing the FBI to include men in their definition of rape, which previously excluded male victims. Its ideology has pushed society to move beyond gender stereotypes and has advocated for men to pursue careers that were deemed as feminine, such as elementary school teaching and social work. It also pushed society to take men's mental health seriously.

Without the work of many feminist scholars, particularly Black women, this book would not be possible—I am only continuing and contributing to a conversation that they started a long time ago.

Our need for feminism comes from the existence of *patriarchy*. When we talk about patriarchy, it's important to know that we're referring to something that's even larger than who heads the household and who does the cooking and cleaning, which are things that individuals can figure out in their own relationships and partnerships. When I reference patriarchy, I'm talking about a whole social system built on men maintaining dominance, holding power, and being viewed as superior to women, therefore asserting the right to abuse, control, and oppress.

Our patriarchal world is structured by these harmful and inequitable beliefs and ideas about the roles of men and women. These beliefs, in turn, shape the rules that we live by.

This is where *masculinity* comes into play.[4] Masculinity and femininity are the rule books given to men and women that detail how they should look and behave. These rules are often framed as being biological, but they are actually socially constructed, meaning that they were determined by society or members of a culture.

One of the impacts of living in a patriarchal world is the practice of gendering values and characteristics in order to keep upholding patriarchy. For example, our society deems qualities like strength, leadership, and aggression as characteristics that only males are born with because this "rule" helps men to keep the power imbalance intact—this is how certain characteristics come to be seen as "masculine." Patriarchal masculinity or toxic masculinity, then, refers to a masculinity that perpetuates authority and hostility and that often contributes to social issues such as violence, misogyny, and sexual assault.

I tend to use the term *patriarchal masculinity* in place of *toxic masculinity* as a way of broadening the conversation. When some men hear *toxic masculinity*, they may think that it means masculinity itself is toxic or that men are bad. But there are many different types of masculinities, and patriarchal masculinity is just one of them. It's important to clarify that both men and masculinity have the potential to be beautiful and *are* beautiful. While the dominant expression of masculinity in our society may uphold patriarchy, masculinity can be expressed in healthy and loving ways. What I hope this book teaches you is that we can own our own authentic versions of masculinity.

---

4. In this book, I will be using the term *masculinity* to describe dominant culture, specifically US and Black masculinity. It is crucial to note that there is not one kind of masculinity, but rather various forms of masculinities that exist around the world, shaped by a range of factors such as region, culture, religion, and more.

To connect these three definitions, here's another way to think of this:

Patriarchy is the social system that places men above women.

Masculinity and femininity are the socially constructed characteristics, behaviors, and roles that dictate how men and women *should* be.

Feminism as an ideology asks us to critique, question, and reexamine what our society has considered to be masculine and feminine, with the larger goal of seeking justice and liberation.

THE BEAUTY OF STORIES

In my journey to find out who I am, what has aided me the most are stories.

I wrote this book because I believe that there are stories from childhood and beyond that need to be told. One of the results of society teaching us that men should be stoic is the difficulty it has created for men to open up, making men live life in silence. What I needed most in my adolescence was for more men to tell their stories. I needed to hear men talk about how they were navigating rejection, loneliness, and insecurity. I needed to hear them talk about not liking what they saw when they looked in the mirror and dealing with traumas from their past.

When I sat down to write this book, I decided that I would tell these stories in hopes that it would make people feel safer to acknowledge their own, whether they decided to tell theirs or not.

My goal is not to tell anyone how they should be a man, but to encourage all of us to examine our beliefs about manhood and masculinity. If we were to challenge societal norms about masculinity, we would realize that these norms limit boys and men in their ability to both give and receive love. When masculinity is associated with traits like toughness, independence, and other patriarchal character-istics, it erodes the capacity for love. In some ways, I see this book as a love letter to men and masculine folks—though it may not be written in letter format, on each page, there is a note somewhere that tells men that who they are to their core is precious and beautiful. Yet, the rules of masculinity that we live by, in many ways, function to keep that beauty and uniqueness hidden.

I wrote this book for anyone who may be struggling on their jour-ney to discover who they are, and also for those who know who they are but find it challenging to live authentically. For the boys who have always felt like they were "different." For the men who have silently endured pain, and for those who were never able to fully embrace themselves. I wrote this book for the empowerment of girls and women, as well as for the healing of all.

I wrote this book because I believe what the nine-year-old boy said is true:

Without the "Man Box," all of us would be free.

HOW TO READ THIS BOOK

Within the pages of this book, you'll find two distinctive sections among the stories: a pause-and-reflect section and a devotional sec-tion. The pause-and-reflect is a moment to engage and interact with what you have just read. You might disagree with some of my analy-ses and perspectives on masculinity, and that is completely okay. Take what you need, and leave everything else. Use the pause-and-reflect section as a way not just to skim through the stories and content, but also to get curious about what this book might be uncovering in your own life and journey.

A devotional is typically a daily reading that combines stories and reflections on biblical texts. Each chapter of this book includes a devotional, but it's important to note that *this is not a Christian book* and should not be approached as such.

You may question, "Then why include it?"

It's complicated. The "Man Box" isn't the only box that exists within our culture. For every identity that we hold, we are placed in another box that works to limit and restrict us. When our identities interact, they create a uniquely beautiful experience. As I wrote this book, I wanted to show what can be discovered when we allow our identities to intersect. In my line of work as a diversity, equity, and inclusion practitioner, we always talk about the importance of authenticity and bringing our fullest self with us. This can't be done when we are forced to leave certain identities at the door.

In part, these devotionals are a form of resistance to patriarchal thinking and a beautiful way to explore masculinity.

Without a doubt, my faith and spiritual practice have shaped me into the person I am today—those who know me know that I love Jesus, and that my Black church upbringing is an important part of my cultural identity. As I began my exploration of masculinity, I realized that the church was one of the many places where these rules about patriarchal masculinity were taught and enforced. I grappled with the way that the church (as a whole) used scriptures to justify violence against women, and to force women into obedience to the authority of all men. These made me search the scriptures to actually get a better picture of what "biblical manhood" is and what the Bible says about patriarchy and masculinity. Though the Bible is typically seen as a text that works to uphold patriarchy, I was surprised by all the ways the Bible challenged this very system, and I wanted to share these learnings as a way to heal the wounds the church has created for some, but also as a way of examining patriarchy through a unique lens.

The devotional section gives readers an opportunity to examine and question how an ancient society grappled with the rules they lived by, many of which were created by their cultural expectations of gender. Its setting in a culture likely more patriarchal than our own allows us to see how patriarchal thinking has been consistent from ancient times to now, and how different people resisted this system to create a world where everyone can be free.

Regardless of whether you identify as Christian, follow another spiritual practice or religion, or simply don't have one, I am confident that there is something valuable in these sections for everyone to glean and reflect on. As you get ready to take this journey, my hope is that you will approach it with an open heart and an open mind.

PAUSE & REFLECT

How would you define a "real man"?

I

SHAME

"Patriarchal masculinity was a standard I could not reach in my young natural flamboyance. It was hard to connect and be in community with men without the hyper-performance or socialization of masculinity in various spaces like school, church, and at home.

I was taught a real man was manly in all of his ways. Never showed weakness, had a disdain for femininity outside of sexual domination, and, most importantly, ultimately valued the ideals of other cishet men."

CHRIS JOSEPH, PHOENIX, AZ

"I'M POSITIVE"

The foundation of a masculine identity based in patriarchy is shame.

I sat with this statement, reading it over and over again, wondering if it was too strong for the first sentence of a book. But it's also a truth. One that cannot be sugarcoated or kept as a "'surprise'" for the end. Masculinity is a cord braided with shame—and for every issue I discuss in this book, we will find shame somewhere. Shame is the emotion that arises from a belief that you are bad, flawed, or not good enough. This feeling typically occurs after we have done something wrong, been embarrassed, or been humiliated. It is often confused with guilt—the sorrow or remorse we feel after we have done something wrong. But guilt is about our actions, while shame is about our identity.

This is what makes shame such a powerful emotion: its connection to who we are and how we perceive ourselves. Because of its personal nature, even though we may struggle to define it, we all know how it feels.

I'll give you a very vulnerable example.

The year 2021 taught me a valuable lesson: Avoid going to the doctor on Fridays because if you receive bad news, you may have to wait until Monday to hear from your doctor again. I learned this lesson the hard way. During my yearly physical (which I urge all men to get if they are able to do so), they took my blood to test for all the usual things—STDs, diabetes, cholesterol, etc. I felt confident and had no worries about the tests. After leaving the doctor's office, I received my results, sat on the couch, and scrolled through each lab test. I was barely paying attention to the details, treating it more like a terms and conditions page, glancing over each result, assuming that everything was normal.

Then I saw it: "Hepatitis C screen: positive."

I blinked, hoping that in the quick instance of opening my eyes, I would see something different.

"Destyn, your hepatitis C screen is positive. This may be a false positive, I am waiting for the titer to return to fully evaluate this. It should take a few days, and I will touch base with you."

Transparently, I didn't even know what hepatitis C was, but I knew from the tone of the message that it was something I didn't want to have. Instantly, I started doing some Googling in an attempt to discover what was going on with me.

"It's curable … phew," was my first reaction. Once I found out that it was curable, I didn't feel the need to tell anyone. I could keep this between myself, my doctor, and my girlfriend. I find it interesting that my first instinct was to hide and to be as discreet as possible.

As I did more research and learned how people contracted it, my desire to conceal it only grew. My eyes widened as I read that it could be passed through sharing drug-injected equipment or by having sex with an infected person, more often among men who have sex with men.

Possibilities and scenarios looped around in my head as I started to imagine what people were going to think about me if they found out. Would they think that I'd been using drugs? Or even what felt worse— would they think that I was gay? These questions eventually turned into declarations about my identity: I'm so stupid. I'm dirty. I'm worthless.

Throughout that entire weekend, I barely ate. Shame destabilized me—and as it grew, so did my anxiety, negative self-talk, and the belief that I was unworthy of love.

Monday finally arrived—the resolution to what had felt like the longest weekend of my life. In the afternoon I received a notification that there was a new message from my doctor. "Destyn, your confirmatory test for hepatitis C was negative. It was likely a false positive or a resolved infection."

I tossed my phone and wept.

PAUSE & REFLECT

When have you felt shame in your life? How did it make you feel, and what caused it?

WILL THE "REAL MEN" PLEASE STAND UP?

In recent years, it has become increasingly acceptable for men and boys to express themselves in ways that were not traditionally considered masculine. Teenage boys are now painting their nails, men are attending therapy sessions, and boys aren't just wearing blue. This new approach to masculinity has been met with resistance in social and political commentary, which suggests that today's men are not "real men." Social media posts have demanded that we return to the historic "tough and strong" archetype of men who knew how to build houses and who had rough, cracked, and calloused hands—and that man was never me.

As I grew up, I realized that I wouldn't fit into this archetype of masculinity that society considered "real." I was too curious as a child to be placed in a box—I wanted to explore a little bit of everything. As I explored my interests, I found myself drawn to dance. My older brother TaDarrean introduced me to Michael Jackson, and I instantly became captivated by his moonwalk and heel-toe steps. I still remember hearing "Billie Jean" for the first time. The music seemed to vibrate throughout my body, as if the instruments were playing inside of me. I wanted to be like MJ, and nothing could convince me that I couldn't master his moves. In secret, I would shut my door, close my eyes, and dance for hours on end, lost in the freedom of movement. I would twirl in circles, kick my feet in the air, and per-form—with no desire to hold back.

As time passed, my love for dance became complicated. Although no one explicitly told me, "You can't be a dancer," I sensed that there was something taboo about it. My parents never forbade me from dancing, but I had an unspoken feeling that it was somehow disap-proved of or at odds with societal expectations. What I did know was that boys who danced on TV were often portrayed as feminine, and at school they were teased as "gay"—two labels that assign boys to the lowest levels of the social hierarchy. As a result, I gradually danced less and less, convinced that it wasn't what "real men" did.

Masculinity functions like a rule book, dictating a code of conduct for men to follow. It dictates how one should speak, from the tone of one's voice to the words used. For so many years of my life, I would force my voice to be deeper when I was around other men. I would probably swear a bit more and make more sexually suggestive jokes because that's what I learned "real men" were supposed to do. Accord-ing to this code of conduct, one is also given guidance on how to walk: It is never okay for your hips to sway even slightly, and you never want your feet to hit the ground too gracefully or you'd be considered soft. This imaginary book teaches us that we should keep a poker face and limit the expression of all emotions—except for anger or rage.

When we don't meet the criteria or if we're not "man enough," we are told that there's something wrong with who we are and that this "something" (no matter what it is) makes us unworthy of belonging and being loved. This is how shame manifests, and it is why shame often leads to insecurity and a lack of self-worth. When we internal-ize the belief that we are unworthy of love, we stop believing that we deserve love from others. In one of my favorite novels, *The Perks of Being a Wallflower*, by Stephen Chbosky, the main character, a freshman in high school, asks his English teacher why he and everyone he loves choose people who treat them as if they are insignificant after witnessing abuse in his older sister's relationship. The teacher responds with the most quoted line from the book:

"We accept the love we think we deserve."[5]

When children are shamed for not fitting perfectly into masculine or feminine categories (which exist on a spectrum), they may struggle to see themselves as loveable, which has serious impacts on their social, emotional, and cognitive development.

As I've studied youth development, I've found that our society is obsessed with raising young people to be miniature versions of someone else. We place our male children in Boy Scouts, in sports programs, and encourage them to engage in rough play because we want to ensure that they will be "man enough" to be one of the "real men." A patriarchal parent's deepest worry for their boy child is centered around how masculine their son will be, rather than how whole they will be. When we shift from "how masculine" to "how whole," we shift from raising children to be who we want them to be and instead assist them in becoming who they already are.

The challenge, however, is unlearning that who they are, and who we are, is shameful.

---

5. Stephen Chbosky, *The Perks of Being a Wallflower*, (New York: Simon & Schuster, 1999).

MASCULINITY & TEARS

I grew up as a mama's boy and a crybaby. Anytime my big brother got slightly too rough with me or anytime I had to stay somewhere without someone I knew, I cried. As I got older, I felt more and more shame for shedding these tears. I started to believe that I was over-emotional and too weak to be with the "big boys"—the precursor of "real men." I made the choice to stop crying when I was in the fourth grade, a moment that I now see as one of the greatest losses of my life.

I was starting a new school and transitioning from a private school to a public school. I was excited, anxious, a little afraid—and like any nine-year-old going somewhere for the first time, I was nervous. On the school bus, I remember reminding myself that I wouldn't cry that day, that I would be strong and courageous. I didn't shed a tear on that first day, and I don't think I ever cried in school again. On one hand, it's great that I made it through the rest of my schooling without crying, but the issue is that the tears were never the real problem. The real problem was my anxiety. Instead of learning how to cope with my anxiety, I learned to suppress the outward display of emotions that revealed them. I mastered the art of controlling tears but never addressed the root cause behind them.

This mindset has followed me into my adult life—don't address the root of the problem, just find a way to hide or cover up the existence of the problem. It's hard for men to cry because from the time we were babies, we were taught to hide or cover it up—to get up whenever we fell, to be told, "You're fine!" whenever we cried, to be told we were just being dramatic if our boyhood tears lasted too long.

To suggest that men don't cry is to suggest that men aren't human. I often wonder what happens to the tears we prevent from flowing and cleansing our faces. Perhaps these tears don't actually disappear but rather begin to flow out in different forms and with different emotions. What if the emotions of rage we feel in our bodies are not rooted in anger but in the old tears that rise within us? What if our frustration is not a sense of being overwhelmed, but a recognition of the many tears residing in us, yearning for release? The grossly ironic nature of shame is that we often experience it in response to things that are natural. The avoidance of tears reflects a denial of the depth of the human experience.

Our shame of tears is directly connected to patriarchy's expectations of men. Patriarchal thinking views men as strong, king-like figures who rule the world and who only exist to serve, honor, and protect his citizens. In an effort to protect his people from the attacks of other kingdoms, a king must always show that he is strong, confident, and unafraid to fight. To publicly show fear, sensitivity, too much kindness, or sadness would make his kingdom vulnerable to attack. While this logic may make some sense in combat, it should not inform how we live our daily lives.

From a patriarchal perspective, bravery and courage are often depicted as the prince saving the princess from monsters or "bad guys." However, I have found that what is just as brave and courageous, if not more, is living authentically and being true to ourselves every day.

The true beauty of embracing vulnerability and compassion is how it often leads to the realization that many of our experiences are shared by others. Whether we are grappling with body insecurity, sexual issues like erectile dysfunction and performance anxiety, health conditions such as high blood pressure and diabetes, mental health issues, loneliness, or any other struggles, there are numerous men who can attest to experiencing the same challenges.

If more men told their stories, we would realize that there's nothing to be ashamed of because these challenges are a part of our collective experience as humans.

PAUSE & REFLECT

How have you been taught to view your tears? Do you see them as negative, positive, or shameful? What influenced these beliefs?

OVERCOMING SHAME

The greatest challenge in overcoming shame is finding the courage to replace it with the truth. When a child accidentally breaks something, their initial reaction is to hide it. They gather the broken pieces, try to hide them in a place where they think no one will find them, and may even use their own bodies to block what they hope adults will not see. They hide it because they feel guilty and may even believe that the accident makes them a bad person.

Although they make every effort to conceal their actions, the truth always catches up with them. Just like how our own secrets have a way of finding the pathway to light. When a parent discovers the broken vase or shattered glass, more often than not their response is, "It's okay. Accidents happen," along with a warm embrace. In that moment, the child realizes that they are not bad; they are simply human.

Thinking back to my hepatitis C scare, what helped me the most was knowing that I was still loved by my then-girlfriend, now wife, Netta. I was waiting for the moment when she would reject me, walk away, or ghost me as if I were now a curse. But she didn't do that. She was gentle with me, never making me feel judged. She affirmed that we would figure this out together, and that everything would be okay. I've found that when I feel ashamed about something, it's so important to tell someone as soon as I can. Having safe people in my life whom I can call and say, "Hey, this thing happened," or, "Hey, I feel like I'm a bad person because…" allows someone else to challenge my shame. These friends never hesitate to remind me of who I am.

I often played this role as a voice to challenge shame when I worked as a college advisor. Students often came into my office, sometimes crying, because they felt defeated by their test scores. "Destyn, I just don't think I'm smart enough for college," many of them would say. My response was always to remind them that they are indeed smart enough, and that they are being challenged—which is a good thing. With that challenge comes learning and figuring things out, and failure is a natural part of the process.

When we don't have someone safe, a friend or therapist, to remind us of who we are or to help us reframe our negative self-talk, we can always turn to ourselves. We all need a list of affirmations to keep in our back pocket or in our phone's Notes app to remind us of who we are and to help us declare our worthiness when we're feeling low.

In our moments of shame, whether it stems from our actions, frightening lab results, or not meeting others' expectations, what we need most is to humanize ourselves and affirm that it's okay, life happens, and who we are is beautiful. This voice is shame's biggest enemy. Through our own voice, we have the power to be radically honest with ourselves.

With our voice, we get to tell our stories the way that we would like them to be told.

DEVOTIONAL

While in the Garden of Eden, Adam and Eve wandered the garden, tending to it and making sure all the plants and crops yielded what they needed. A beautiful aspect of the culture was that "[they] were both naked, the man and his wife, and were not ashamed" (Genesis 2:25, KJV). An interesting point to note from this scripture is that in God's original plan, our bodies were not something we were supposed to be ashamed of. Imagine a world where the beauty of our bodies could be acknowledged without the risk of being objectified or sexualized. After being tempted by a serpent and eating the fruit from the tree of knowledge of good and evil, everything changed forever. From a Christian worldview, this is the moment when sin entered the world, and due to their disobedience, their perfect world now knew the reality of evil.

After eating the fruit, "the eyes of them both were opened, and they knew that they were naked; and they sewed fig leaves together, and made themselves aprons" (Genesis 3:7, KJV). Here, we see the same effect that shame has on us—our first instinct is to cover up. The most interesting aspect we learn from this passage is the way they initially had no concept of nakedness. Their nudity was natural to them until it wasn't. Then Adam and Eve heard the sound of God walking in the garden and did what any of us would have done—hid in plain sight. God called out to them, "Where are you?" In Christian theology, we hold the belief that God is omniscient, meaning all-knowing. In this case, God didn't ask where they were out of ignorance; rather, the question was for Adam and Eve to ponder, not to tell God. Adam's response to God was, "I heard thy voice in the garden, and I was afraid, because I was naked; and I hid myself." God responded by asking a powerful question, "Who told you that you were naked?" (Genesis 3:10–11, ASV).

This question that God asked Adam and Eve has been a framework for how I navigate shame. In this passage, God is teaching Adam and Eve something significant about the nature of shame—it usually comes from outside of us. When I feel shame in my body and engage in negative self-talk, I have started the practice of asking myself, "Who told you that?" When something happens that makes me feel like I'm not good enough or not worthy to have a seat at the table, I ask myself, "Who told you that you weren't worthy? Who told you that you didn't deserve to have a seat at this table?" That question always gets me to pause and think about the sources of such messaging. By identifying the source, I can acknowledge that the message didn't come from within, nor did it come from God.

When we meditate on who God told us we are, we remember that *we are accepted*: "Therefore, accept each other just as Christ has accepted you so that God will be given glory" (Romans 15:7, ASV);

we remember that *we are chosen*: "I brought you from the ends of the earth and called you from its farthest corners. I said to you: You are my servant; I have chosen you; I haven't rejected you" (Isaiah 41:9, ASV);

and *we are deeply loved*: "For I am convinced that neither death nor life, neither angels nor demons, neither the present nor the future, nor any powers, neither height nor depth, nor anything else in all creation, will be able to separate us from the love of God that is in Christ Jesus our Lord" (Romans 8:38–39, ASV).

Regardless of the faith tradition you may come from, an important practice for our overall well-being is to examine where the beliefs about yourself come from. We don't have to accept every message that seeks to make its way to the core of our identity. Words spoken with intent to shame can be rejected by internally responding to it with declarations of who we are.

PAUSE & REFLECT

In which areas of your life do you currently feel shame? What might you do or tell yourself to reaffirm your true identity?

II

IMAGE

"As a young boy, I was taught that my body was a vessel for performance. In sports, 'putting it all on the line' was not just a euphemism—my value as a man was earned on the field and in the weight room. I demanded far too much of my body, and that lesson is now inscribed across my body as surgical scars and shame.

As I reckon with stiff joints and chronic pain, I caution men to be kind to their bodies, and create a world which teaches us that existing in our own skin is enough."

JOHN FELDKAMP, CINCINNATI, OH

PICTURE PERFECT

Transparently, I'm not really into taking pictures.

The sight of every flash and sound of every shutter always leaves me with a slightly icky feeling. The joy of taking pictures was stripped away by an insecurity I've held since I was a child. As a boy who never quite fit the masculine prototype well, the biggest thing I missed out on was participating in sports. I never really thought about how that would make my life different until I started to see my friends' bodies drastically change. While the other boys developed muscles and abs, I watched my own body develop curves and fluff. I watched the girls ask to touch their six-packs and feel their biceps, and I became jealous.

This started a journey of hyper-focusing on what my body looked like, especially in pictures. To this day, the first thing I look at when I see a picture of myself is my body. I search to see if my "man boobs" are showing, how broad my shoulders look, and if whatever I am wearing makes me look slimmer. I was convinced that "real men" had a certain body—a real man had a muscular physique. This wasn't just some idea in my head but was confirmed all around me. The body of every superhero, pop star, and leader was slender and White.

In the patriarchy, a certain type of body is seen as superior and reinforced by capitalistic culture. From boyhood, advertisements and the media want us to believe that if we have rock-hard abs and are ripped, our lives will be easier. There would be no protein powders, gym memberships, and male enhancement pills if our body image wasn't treated as the source of our problems. Every product marketed to young boys and men sells the idea that this deodorant, cologne, workout routine, or watch will fix "it," neglecting the fact that often the "it" is our own struggle with finding the courage to be who we are.

Additionally, power and privilege in our society are distributed based on these physical attributes. For example, there is a standard body type that is considered when building airplanes, roller coasters, and office chairs, and this standard type certainly leaves out and excludes larger and smaller bodies, or bodies that have various abilities. Not only does the patriarchy prioritize certain body types, it is also built to cater to those bodies, leaving others out of the picture.

Throughout my journey, I have often struggled to find a balanced view of my body. How do I acknowledge the clear power dynamics related to body and appearance and balance them with my personal feelings about my own body? How do I embrace the body I have that society has told me is not desirable or beautiful?

PAUSE & REFLECT

Describe the physical attributes, personality traits, and achievements that you deem essential for someone to be considered an ideal man in your eyes.

IDENTITY, IMAGE & THE PHALLUS

In order to understand the source of my image insecurities, I have to open back up the box that masculinity placed me in. The last chapter discussed how this box of masculinity shapes our characteristics, interests, and expressions of emotions. The rule book doesn't stop there but continues to describe in detail what is expected of a man in terms of his image—how tall he is, the style of his hair, the color of his skin, and how big his "manhood" is.

The way we see ourselves (our image) is influenced by our identity: our religion, socioeconomic status, race, ethnicity, gender, sexual orientation, age, etc. As a light-skinned Black man, I have benefited directly from colorism. Because my shade of Black is often viewed as the most attractive, this has led to seeing people of my complexion always represented in film and music videos, often as the love interest. My complexion in many ways gave me more confidence, and at the same time it also gave me insecurity. Light-skinned Black men also carry a reputation for being soft and feminine. And though some of these things are jokes in my community, these jokes had real implications. The light-skinned boys were the pretty boys, and the pretty boys were too pretty to fight or play rough.

Our perceptions of our bodies are shaped by our personal experiences, and even generational and historical traumas. Since being forced from our ancestral lands and enslaved across the Americas, Black bodies have been dehumanized and objectified. When our ancestors were sold into slavery, they were stripped of their dignity and forced to display their bodies as commodities, with White slave owners assessing and exploiting them as if they were mannequins. As they firmly grasped their arms, evaluating the muscle tone and strength, and examined their teeth to see the age and health of each one, the strongest most well-built slaves were deemed the most valuable.

This same dehumanization continued in literature, media, and advertisements that sought to portray Black men and Black masculinity as animalistic, dangerous, and uncivilized. These portrayals were designed to instill fear in White men who saw Black masculinity as a threat to White masculinity and Whiteness. Hundreds of years later, with the abolishment of slavery, these depictions of Black bodies still remain. Much of the professional sports industry still has a similar view of Black bodies, reinforcing the idea that

Black male athletes are useful when tamed and under the supervision of Whiteness.[6]

One of my favorite episodes on my podcast *Rethinking Manhood* was a discussion I had with one of my Hmong American friends about Asian American masculinity and penis sizes. In that conversation, we delved into how Asian American men are often portrayed in the media as geeky or unattractive and are rarely cast as the love interest in shows. This led to an intriguing conversation about the desexualization of Asian men and the oversexualization of Black men, topics that ultimately center around the fixation on penis size.

A characteristic of patriarchal masculinity is power—and the penis is one of its symbols. It is not accidental that *manhood* is one of the names we have given to the penis. The societal belief is that the bigger the penis, the more manly someone is. Perhaps this is why many men have the disturbing habit of sending unsolicited pictures of their genitals on dating apps and websites (which is a form of sexual harassment that needs to stop *immediately*). Society has taught men that their penises are the most valuable aspect of themselves, and that based on its size and girth, it has the potential to bring them love, sex, and acceptance.

In the same way that patriarchy compels individuals to prove they are "man enough" from adolescence to adulthood, many men also grapple with concerns of if they are "big enough." This topic remains taboo for many men, as discussing it would require them to disclose their own lack of self-confidence. Furthermore, insecurity is often characterized as a feminine issue, something that we believe only women or non-masculine folks experience.

6. Gary Sailes, *African Americans in Sports* (London: Routledge, Taylor & Francis Group, 2017).

To admit one's insecurity is to be vulnerable, an emotion that the rule book has prohibited.

PAUSE & REFLECT

How do societal expectations regarding race and body image impact your perception of yourself and your identity?

INSECURITY & VULNERABILITY

When we feel insecure about our bodies or anything else, our human instinct is to find a way to cover it up or hide it, as we have learned. We hide behind things like "gym bro" social media culture, which often involves flaunting physical strength to overcompensate for other insecurities. We continue to hide by wearing expensive clothing and accessories, constantly one-upping each other, or by bragging about how much sex we have and who we have it with. While covering ourselves up may feel most natural and comfortable, it's a never-ending cycle that never fully satisfies us. All the sex in the world or having the body we desire will not solve all of our insecurities. Instead of overcompensating or being ostentatious, we can choose to be vulnerable and allow ourselves to be open and exposed, leading to the possibility of being seen and known by others—and even more intimately by ourselves.

One of the most liberating and empowering experiences I've had with my body was doing a shirtless photo shoot.

While working on a social media post for *Rethinking Manhood* about patriarchal masculinity and body image, I had a brilliant idea—or so I thought at the time. I wanted to convey my personal struggle with body image in a more tangible way, rather than just writing about my experiences. I decided to take a bold approach and came up with the idea of ending my thread with a shirtless photo of myself. After making this decision, I set up my tripod, opened my windows, poured a glass of wine, and began taking these shirtless portraits. I'll be honest—for the first fifteen minutes, it was incredibly awkward. I told myself not to think about the results and to simply have fun. As the photo shoot continued and as the sun beamed into my apartment, I was awestruck. It had been so long since I'd been shirtless outdoors that I'd forgotten the sensation of the sun meeting my chest, and the warmth of its rays on my exposed skin. The only word that captured the feeling was *free*. I was breaking the rules, and I had no idea that deviance could feel so liberating.

As my impromptu photo shoot came to a close, I scrolled through the pictures on my phone and found some that made me proud and others that made me cringe. When it came time to include a picture in my post, I chickened out.

Even though I didn't follow through with the original plan, I realized at that moment that vulnerability isn't just about how we open up to others but also about how we are open with ourselves. Although the pictures were never posted, I still became more comfortable with my body the way it was on that particular day. This doesn't mean that my insecurities were erased, or that I never thought about my body again, no. But it was a healthy step in embracing who I am.

When it comes to acknowledging an insecurity and being vulnerable about it, in my experience taking small steps is the best approach. The all-or-nothing thinking that stems from patriarchy can make us believe that a "real man" must dive in headfirst or jump straight into the deep end. Learning to be vulnerable is like learning to swim—before you can fully submerge yourself in the water, you have to first get comfortable putting your feet in. Then, you work toward standing in the water and getting accustomed to its presence around you. Embracing my body meant starting with small steps like checking my weight less frequently, buying clothes that actually fit, and learning to appreciate all the many things this body can do.

Our body and physical features play a huge role in shaping how we are perceived by others, and it would be unfair to treat them like they are meaningless. And yet, regardless of how I feel about my body or the goals I set for its appearance, I remind myself that feeling great about my body and looking the way I would like it to does not guarantee what we all seek—to be loved, known, and accepted. While patriarchal ideologies may lead us to believe that this can be achieved through the size of our penises or the strength of our arms, please remember that the path to being loved, known, and accepted begins with vulnerability—opening yourself up to be seen by yourself, and others.

DEVOTIONAL

Throughout the Bible, there are many scriptures that challenge us to expand the way we see our bodies. In 2 Corinthians 5:1–8, physical bodies are compared to temporary tents that house us while we live on earth but will eventually be replaced in heaven by a new home that will last forever. Seeing the body as a temporary home can be a powerful metaphor when we apply it to body image because it forces us to ask the question: Who do these temporary tents house, and how do we describe them apart from the tent?

In Genesis 2:7, Adam was formed from the dust—but it wasn't until God's breath was breathed into Adam's nostrils that he became "a living soul" (KJV). While our bodies and souls are connected, the two are not interdependent, meaning that even when our bodies decay, our souls will not. George Macdonald puts it this way, "You don't have a soul. You are a Soul. You have a body."[7] Beyond our bodies, we are the thoughts that we think, and the thoughts that shape the emotions we feel, and the experiences that our emotions give life to. While our bodies constantly change as our smooth skin gets promoted to wrinkles, and our brown and black hairs elevate to grays, our souls are also changing with growths in wisdom and new learnings.

When we look in the mirror, it's easy to become clouded by our appearance, seeing it as a reflection of who we are, when really it is just one piece of the picture. Without our personhood, that picture is incomplete. Acknowledging this can give us more compassion for our bodies and help us to shift away from constantly judging ourselves.

---

7. George MacDonald, *Annals of a quiet neighbourhood* (London: Hurst and Blackett, 1867).

Whenever I don't like the way my body looks, I push myself to gratitude—giving thanks for what my body can do, and for the way it allows my inner person to touch, smell, listen, taste, and see. This neutral perspective on the body can also be in harmony with celebrating how it looks the way it is, acknowledging that the bodies we're born with were called beautiful by the Creator of the universe.

In Genesis 1:31, God looks at everything He created and says that it is all "very good" (ASV). What I love about this verse in Genesis is its reminder that the first word used to describe humanity is *good*. I appreciate the emphasis on humanity's goodness because it challenges the human tendency to view people through a lens of deficiency, defining them by what they lack rather than what they have. I often think this tendency pushes us further away from experiencing and expressing love. Without a doubt, labels are powerful, and we see their power magnified in the ways that we treat people whom society has labeled as "bad." Our moral comfort with the inhumane and dehumanizing conditions of prisons is based on the labels the criminal justice system has given those who are incarcerated. But regardless of who we are and what we do, I always find joy in knowing that God's eyes are powerful enough to look beyond our mistakes and faults and still see goodness. Which leads to an important question: What do your eyes see when they look at people?

God's outlook on us as humans is found in one of my favorite scriptures, Psalm 139:14, which says that we are "fearfully and wonderfully made" (KJV). The phrase *fearfully* doesn't suggest that we were created to live in fear, but rather to be regarded with awe and wonder. It's like the breathtaking moment when a bride walks down the aisle in a stunning white gown, leaving those who witness it speechless in the presence of such beauty. We've been conditioned to only see this kind of awe and wonder in women, but here God is challenging this notion by exclaiming that His eye sees this in every human on the earth.

In the Christian faith, both beauty and delight are found in all humans because they were all made by a creative God who created them in His image. If God was not a creator, perhaps He would have given everyone brown eyes. But instead, He chose to gift some with brown, some with blue, some with hazel, and others with hues that shift like the changing light. Similarly, our bodies were designed in diverse ways. Some were made to offer comfort through their hugs, which can communicate love more effectively than words; others have the strength to lift heavy things; some have legs built for speed; and others move with a slower, yet more graceful, rhythm.

Our relationship with our bodies is complex and exists on a spectrum. Whether we accept, reject, love, or hate them, the reminder that we are more than our physical bodies and the belief that our bodies are good regardless of their weight, length, or form can both work together to help us cultivate a balanced view of who we are.

PAUSE & REFLECT

What could be the first step toward embracing greater vulnerability toward your body?

III

ANGER

*"Anger has been a constant companion from my earliest memories—
and so has my hatred of it. I was raised to view my anger as an
irredeemable part of my personality and identity, and I was also told
that anger is a sin. Of course, anything sinful deserved vilification, so
anger was framed as something to be hated. As a tender-hearted boy
who felt emotions deeply, I thought my anger was a core part of me.*

*Thus, hatred of my anger meant that I hated a part of myself. In
adulthood I've only recently started the healing process by making space
for my anger—understanding my experience with it instead of suppressing
it. Through years of personal work and restorative relationship with others,
I have concluded that maybe anger isn't as simple as I was led to believe."*

ALAN GAY, CLEVELAND, OH

MY FIRST FIGHT

My heart pounded as the word echoed in my ears. The
sound of my heartbeat rang loudly, racing almost as fast
as my mind. The boy had said the word, the word that I

would hear many times after, but this would be one of the first times I'd heard it directed at me. "Nigger," he said to me, or maybe it was, "Nigga," but the difference did not matter coming from his brown hair, blue eyes, and thin lips. I felt something rise up in my body that felt like heat, slowly moving from the soles of my shoes to the top of my head. As that heat intensified, I did what I was taught to do—I struck him. I pushed his face onto the desk and seized him in a headlock from behind.

In my own ignorance, I failed to think about what he was feeling at that moment. I held his throat a bit longer than what would have been considered socially acceptable as my eyes scanned the room for spectators, seeing the fear in their eyes and their desperation to find a teacher. Then I let him go.

After the fight, I received two days of in-school suspension, and he received nothing. I was told that I was overreacting, and that it was not okay to hit someone, even if they called you a word that has dehumanized your people for generations. *Whatever*, I remember thinking to myself as I left the principal's office and waited for my parents to pick me up. Life was a bit different after that moment, especially in the way that I saw my anger and my own capacity to express it.

PAUSE & REFLECT

When was the first time you remember losing control due to anger? Can you recount the incident that led to this loss of control and reflect on why you believe you reacted in that manner?

REFRAMING OUR ANGER

While serving my in-school suspension, I found myself contemplating how to suppress or avoid my anger, rather than learning to manage it. I was reminded of this memory recently when I found myself getting angry during a social and political debate with a person I had just met. As the conversation touched on emotionally charged topics with tangible real-life consequences, including matters of life and death, tensions ran high. My emotions grew stronger, and my voice grew louder and louder. I started to feel the heat rise in my body again, which prompted me to abruptly walk away from the conversation. The feelings from my elementary school fight came back up. Just like how my classmates had seen me as a monster, I couldn't help but feel like history was repeating itself, casting me once again as the very monster they perceived me to be.

As I made my way to my car, a heavy wave of remorse washed over me. I couldn't help but ask myself repeatedly, "What have I just done?" This question spiraled into a deep sense of shame as I walked, grappling with self-imposed labels like, "I am bad," and "I am angry," almost bringing me to tears. I reached out to my friend Terra, knowing she wouldn't hesitate to hold me accountable.[8] I provided Terra with a detailed account of the argument, recounting what had been said by both parties. As the conversation continued, I came to the realization that I had never insulted or attacked the other person personally; my anger had showed up solely in the form of my raised voice rather than verbal attacks.

---

8. Men, it's crucial to have someone in your life who deeply cares for you but is willing to challenge you when you're wrong.

Terra's response sparked something in me as she responded to my ramblings with this:

"Destyn, you're allowed to be angry."

I am? I pondered, grappling with the realization and contemplating the rare occasions in my life when I had permitted myself to feel anger.

ANGER & IDENTITY

I began to think about the way I had implicitly been taught that an angry Black man is a dead Black man. I learned quickly in school that you had to be careful about who you raised your voice to, or perhaps who you even looked at funny. This same message comes back up in the ways that I have had to navigate social systems, which result in frustration—and yet, regardless of if a police officer is profiling you or harassing you, or no matter how often he says something racist, you can't get angry. For an angry Black man has two destinations: a cell or a grave.

As societal narratives continue to paint Black men as inherently dangerous, aggressive, and intimidating, I have begun to recognize how deeply ingrained these stereotypes are and how they have influenced my self-perception. I have realized that society does not afford me the same freedom to express anger that it does to others—a realization that troubles me deeply. During a lengthy therapy session dedicated to unpacking this "incident," I expressed my doubts to my White male therapist, questioning whether my introspection was perhaps excessive.

"Maybe this isn't really about the guy you were arguing with but more about you," my therapist said. I responded to his statement with silence, and in my silence, I thought to myself how complex the situation was. My reaction hadn't been just about being challenged by another man who wouldn't budge or listen well. It had been about me feeling the need to prove that I was "man enough" in that moment. I had needed to show him that I was not soft, that I was not afraid of him, and that I was not intimidated by him. As I began to verbalize these thoughts, my therapist listened attentively, nodding his head in understanding. He didn't interrupt me but instead allowed me to keep talking and exploring my feelings. Eventually, he stopped me, not because he didn't want to hear more but because he could see that this level of self-analysis was creating more shame.

"You had a drink or two, and you may have overreacted a little bit—that doesn't make you a bad person," he said. Honestly, his response annoyed me. I thought, *Of course, that's easy for you to say— you're a White man whose mistakes can be humanized or rationalized. Mine are only criminalized.* However, deep down, I knew that what he was saying was true, and I knew that societal views of my Blackness had pushed me into perfectionism as a way of bargaining with White supremacy and showing the world that I was not one of those Black men—instead, I was one of the "good ones."

After our therapy session, I continued to think about Terra's words, "You're allowed to be angry." When Terra, a Black woman, whose anger has been policed, scrutinized, and silenced far more than mine, reminded me that I was allowed to be angry, a significant shift occurred in my perception and comprehension of anger. I came to realize that anger is indeed an essential emotion. Imagine a world where we never get angry. While aspects of such a world may seem appealing, its existence would require the absence of evil, corruption, and oppression.

One of the reasons I believe we have anger is because it is the only natural response to injustice.

Anger serves as a powerful emotion that alerts us when something is off or not aligned with our values. It often arises when our boundaries are violated or when we witness actions that we deem disrespectful or unethical. Our bodies require this emotion to send crucial signals to our brains, and anger can propel us to take necessary action in response to injustice. While recognizing wrongdoing is important, it often takes the heat, intensity, and urgency of anger to empower us to speak out or intervene.

PAUSE & REFLECT

How has your anger influenced your actions? Has it ever led you to do something you regret, or inspired you to take actions you're proud of?

ANGER & PATRIARCHY

Though anger can serve as a catalyst for positive change, it can also be wielded as a tool of patriarchy. The intersection of anger and patriarchy becomes problematic when anger is equated with masculinity.

When I was a graduate student at the University of Minnesota, my research focused on Black masculinity within youth-organized sports programs, examining how sports impact participants' perceptions and conceptions of masculinity and manhood. One notable observation I made was the distinct way in which coaches responded to their youth players expressing anger. When these players became angry during the game, the coaches seemed to appreciate the intensity. They often sought to amplify and sustain this intensity, but somewhere the line between intensity and anger became blurred.

During one of the practices I observed with a basketball team, a young member was not performing well. They were moving slowly and missing their basketball shots, and it was clear that their head wasn't in the game. The coaches and team kept pushing him, even after he expressed feeling unwell: "I think I have to throw up," he told them. The coaches rolled their eyes. When he reached his breaking point, he screamed, "My dad just went back to fucking prison!" and went to the corner of the court and began to cry. The coaches attempted to offer some comfort but ultimately told him that others were going through worse, and he had to keep going. They quickly resumed the practice, hoping that his anger would motivate him to play better.

This mentality goes beyond the court and carries on to other areas of life, promoting the idea that real manhood is synonymous with this form of expression. Undoubtedly, the emotion that society is most comfortable with men displaying is anger. In the workplace, when a man expresses anger, it is often interpreted as drive, passion, and determination. In contrast, when women exhibit the same emotion, they are more likely to be labeled as overly emotional and excessive, or as someone who takes things too seriously.

One of the manifestations of patriarchy's influence on men and masculine individuals is the way in which self-control is perceived. There is a prevailing societal notion that men are unable to control their emotions, behaviors, or desires, particularly in the context of aggression and anger. Male rage is seen as biological or natural, and if that rage leads to violence, it is often excused. We tend to believe that a man's rage is uncontrollable, and if you do something to provoke him, he must react and "teach you a lesson." Each time we hear or utter phrases like, "Boys will be boys," "That's just how guys are," or, "Boys have a natural tendency to be rough," we reinforce the idea that anger and aggression are inherent biological traits of masculinity. This kind of thinking leads us to victim blame others when men are the perpetrators of domestic violence, workplace harassment, or sexual assault, to name a few. These ingrained phrases and beliefs have often shielded men from being held accountable for their harmful actions fueled by anger or spite. In numerous instances, we see the aftermath of male anger manifested as damaged property, physical harm, or destroyed objects and lives. As men, we must be mindful of the ways that we can weaponize our anger, using it to say whatever we want, to do harm, or solely because we can get away with it.

The feminist scholar bell hooks says, "Much of the anger boys express is itself a response to the demand that they not show any other emotions. Anger feels better than numbness because it often leads to more instrumental action. Anger can be, and usually is, the hiding place for fear and pain."[9] In romantic relationships, individuals often have a love–hate relationship with masculine anger. While they may hate what that anger leads them to do, they often find some comfort in seeing their partner show emotion—seeing them angry is better than seeing them stoic. Their anger at least serves as a reminder that they are human. Many of us have resorted to anger as a means of overcompensating for our feelings of insecurity regarding

9. bell hooks, *The Will to Change: Men, Masculinity, and Love* (New York: Simon & Schuster, 2003).

ourselves and our masculinity. There is a mistaken belief that by yelling loudly, punching a wall, or displaying aggression, we are proving our manliness. In this way, anger serves as another mask that we wear. We put on the mask of anger because it is more acceptable to wear than the tears of a mourning heart, the stomachache of anxiety, and the weight of sadness.

FINDING BALANCE IN OUR ANGER

While anger is not inherently negative as an emotion, it is essential for us to approach it mindfully and without self-judgment. We should strive to understand and balance this emotion, finding healthier ways to express it. Certain injustices and events rightfully provoke anger within us, motivating us to take action toward creating a fairer and more equitable world. Whether it is the stories of Black women facing discrimination in the workplace, genocides occurring globally, gun violence, or mass incarceration, these issues should stir a passionate response within us, compelling us to advocate for change.

The key to navigating this difference is understanding and knowing when our anger is constructive or toxic. This distinction can be discovered by observing the actions it leads us to take. Toxic anger is self-centered, leading to a situation where no one else's opinions or emotions are heard or considered important (especially if they come from a woman). This type of anger is displayed when we don't get what we want or when we resist a challenge or change. At its core, it stems from one person's feelings and reactions without regard for anyone else. On the other hand, if our anger motivates us to understand or address a problem or injustice, then it is constructive. The difference here is that a toxic anger will always feed our egos, while a constructive one will feed our desire to create a better world.

As we journey through life, we won't always handle this distinction perfectly, and that's okay. There will be times when our anger is misplaced or directed at the wrong thing or person. In those moments, we should hold ourselves accountable and continue striving to be better, while making sure not to spiral into shame or beat ourselves up for our human response.

When the heat of anger arises, sometimes our response needs to consist of deep breaths, exercise, journal sessions, or processing sessions in therapy. Sometimes our response needs to be drawing, crafting, or creating something. Sometimes we need to take a break, step away, and set boundaries; and there are even times when what we need most is to forgive. And yet, when the flames of injustice rise, we need to act and not stomp on the flames too quickly. We may need to give ourselves time and grace to be moved and refined by the flames, burning ourselves to a point where we become advocates and agents for change.

DEVOTIONAL

One of my favorite moments involving Jesus in the Bible is when he
overturns tables in the temple. These events, which I like to refer to
as "Jesus moments," are instances where Jesus surprises us by doing
what we least expect him to do. It's not just masculinity that we
tend to confine to a box; we often limit people, ideas, denominations, and even our perception of God within narrow boundaries.
We often avoid talking about the Jesus moment found in John 2:14–
15, because it conflicts with the boxes we've placed around anger or
frustration. In our society, we have witnessed abuse and harm stem-
ming from anger, leading to a loss of belief in the existence of a holy
and righteous anger.

In the story, as it is told, "In the temple courts [Jesus] found people selling cattle, sheep and doves, and others sitting at tables exchang-
ing money. So he made a whip out of cords, and drove all from the
temple courts, both sheep and cattle; he scattered the coins of the
money changers and overturned their tables."[10] (John 2:14–15, NIV).
This action challenges the common perception of Jesus as the epitome
of love, kindness, and gentleness, just as our stereotypes of "healthy
masculinity" can be wrongly seen as passive and timid. The key aspect
to consider in this story is Jesus's motivation behind driving people
from the temple and overturning the tables.

The temple is depicted as a sacred place, referenced to in Isaiah
56:7 as a "house of prayer" (ASV). Essentially, this story in John 2 is
about how people were failing to recognize and honor the sanctity
of the temple. The sacredness of the temple was being compromised

---

10. Bible, New International Version (London: Hodder & Stoughton, 2007).

not only by its transformation into a marketplace, but also by the implications of exploitation and mistreatment of individuals. Jesus did not witness this occurrence and ignore it or pretend like he didn't see it. No, he put a stop to it by driving the people away and turning over their tables. While this kind of anger had the right motivations and did not seek to harm, I also read this moment as an act of love. There would be nothing to be angry about if Jesus did not deeply love those who were being exploited, or mistreated, those who were likely poor or foreigners. He was upset because he loved.

The decline in church membership and the departure of many young people from the church may be attributed to the fact that the church sometimes directs its anger at the wrong things. Some church leaders might get upset about introducing a new variety of worship styles or allowing hats in the sanctuary, rather than addressing more pressing issues such as the use of the pulpit to target and marginalize certain groups of people. The church's failure to hold its leaders accountable and its attempts to cover up the assaults and molestations of its members are serious issues that have caused harm and feelings of betrayal within communities. While it is true that not all churches engage in such behavior, there are far too many stories of individuals who have endured toxic, controlling, and abusive leadership. It is a valid question to wonder if Jesus would have flipped over the tables in many modern-day temples, expressing anger at the injustices that have occurred in a place that is meant to be holy and just.

The overturning of tables and cleansing of the temple should not be justification for us to be unkind or easily angered. This was not an instance of exaggerated reactions; it was about upholding holiness and justice. The lesson here is for us to not stand by idly in the face of injustice, but to overturn the tables of corruption, exploitation, and injustice in our homes and communities.

PAUSE & REFLECT

What tables of exploitation and injustice are you called to overturn or confront?

IV

GENTLENESS

"Gentleness means actively listening to someone or oneself while being present and open. When working with youth, I invite them to talk about their concerns by saying, 'Hey, you look upset. Would you like to talk about it?' This approach gives them the agency to choose whether to open up or not.

I learned the importance of gentleness through personal experience, where yelling adults left me feeling resentful and disrespected. I strive to be a gentle and patient role model for youth, showing them that masculinity can be about kindness and empathy, not aggression and impatience."

KYLE THOMPSON, SAINT PAUL, MN

THE EXPECTATION OF AGGRESSION

was never a fighter, yet I have spent my entire life feeling the pressure to be ready to fight if the situation demanded it. In society, boys are often judged based on their willingness to participate in rough play, with an unwritten rule that even in the face of excessive force or unexpected aggression, one must not show any sign of vulnerability. I knew that fighting wasn't for me at an early age, but still felt expected to learn. I can remember the times my brother attempted to teach me the stance, the moves, the tough demeanor. Despite my attempts to emulate him, there was always a discomfort within me when it came to displaying this kind of aggression. There was always something I just couldn't get. I understood that there was a time and a place where it might be necessary, I guess; I understood that there was something important about being able to defend and protect yourself. This, however, didn't feel like that. This was more about learning a tool that I would be forced to use for the rest of my life.

As boys transition into men, they often undergo various social rituals and rites of passage. The first typically involves getting into a physical altercation. The second involves reaching new levels of intimacy with a partner and the ultimate rite of passage: losing one's virginity. These rites are significant in shaping our understanding of masculinity and are reinforced through various forms of media. For example, it is common for many to embrace the belief that a boy who cannot defend himself is ill-prepared for the challenges that lie ahead. This raises questions about the world we are preparing boys to navigate and the assumptions we make about their future. For White boys, I've often seen the socialization to be dominant and aggressive translate to how to dominate the social, political, and business world. For Black boys, I've seen this translate to how to survive harsh conditions of the world—the conditions of the streets or even prison.

Despite my inclination to follow the rules and approach life by the book, one of my deepest fears has always been the prospect of ending up in prison. It may sound surprising, even vulnerable, to admit this. However, since my teenage years, the thought of spending the rest of my life behind bars has spawned anxiety and plagued my worst nightmares. Growing up as a Black boy, narratives in my environment subtly suggested that my future would likely lead to a grave or a cell—a fate confirmed by grim statistics like the oft-repeated "one in three Black men will go to jail."[11] I remember sitting in a classroom, a teacher ominously pointing out this statistic while singling out the Black boys present. This fear has prompted me to ponder its origins and led me to recognize that a significant part of it is rooted in my perception of men—a belief that they are inherently unsafe.

One of the most significant casualties in this journey from boyhood to manhood is the erosion of gentleness.

When baby boys are born, we show them gentleness, constantly holding them, comforting them when they cry, kissing them, and telling them how much we love and care about them. However, as boys grow older, that gentleness turns into "tough love." The hugs become handshakes, and the kisses become distant lips drifting further apart as time goes on. The transition from tender embraces to distant gestures reflects a loss of intimate connection.

When did we stop needing the warmth of being held, kissed, and loved?

---

11. Thomas P. Bonczar, "Prevalence of Imprisonment in the U.S. Population, 1974-2001," Bureau of Justice Statistics, August 2003, https://bjs.ojp.gov/content/pub/pdf/piusp01.pdf.

PAUSE & REFLECT

Can you remember the last time someone referred to you as gentle? Perhaps the last time you've used the word *gentle* as a way of describing yourself?

PROTECTING BLACK WOMEN

The most talked-about moment of the 2022 Academy Awards was the incident between actor Will Smith and comedian Chris Rock. While announcing the nominees for the Best Documentary Feature, Chris Rock made a joke about Will Smith's wife, Jada Pinkett Smith, and her short hair, comparing her to G.I. Jane. Will Smith walked up to Chris Rock on national television during the live broadcast of the awards show and smacked him. He then returned to his seat and shouted, "Keep my wife's name out of your fucking mouth!"

This moment sparked a lot of conversations, especially given Jada Pinkett Smith's openness about her alopecia diagnosis. Many believed that Chris Rock's joke was insensitive and problematic. The discussion that intrigued me the most was about how Will Smith handled the situation. Was he justified in hitting Chris Rock, or was this another example of toxic masculinity? I wonder how social expectations influenced Will Smith's reaction that day. If his wife was being disrespected, he had to consider what his response said about himself in the public eye. If Will Smith didn't intervene or interrupt Chris Rock with violence, would that change how we perceive of him as a man? Would we see him as less masculine for not reacting with violence?

The most common argument I heard in that discourse was that Will was trying to protect Jada. This led me to consider how men define their identity and perceive their role in relationships as the protector. For many men, physical protection is a way to express love, and in romantic partnerships, women often seek men whom they believe can physically protect them from others. In the social commentary surrounding the incident, I saw many people saying that what Will Smith did was what protecting Black women truly means. The issue I have with this interpretation of his actions as "protection" is how we automatically link protection with violence, as if the two are always intertwined.

Looking at protection through a lens of gentleness, we can see that it extends beyond physical defense. Protecting Black women involves examining how the actions and behaviors of men make women feel unsafe, and holding these men, who may be our friends, accountable through dialogue or being a good role model. It also means honoring women and their time, paying them fairly for their work, not allowing them to be silenced, and truly listening to them. Protecting Black women involves recognizing and giving credit for their achievements, and raising sons who are nurturing, respectful, and loving.

From this perspective, boldness and gentleness can coexist. We can courageously call out disrespectful behavior while doing so with care and empathy.

In a patriarchal model, there is an expectation that men are the protectors, but there is also an implicit assumption that men themselves do not need protection. This can create anxiety and pressure for men, as they carry the burden of always having to be ready to fight and defend themselves, often feeling the need to be armed with weapons. If we shift toward a more loving and inclusive society, we would understand that protection should be a collective effort that doesn't solely rely on one gender. It is the responsibility of all individuals to look after, care for, and love one another, regardless of gender. Ultimately, a society based on love and mutual respect would prioritize the well-being and safety of all its members, fostering a culture of support and protection for everyone.

PAUSE & REFLECT

What does it mean to you to be a protector?

RECLAIMING SOFTNESS

For many men and boys, the fear of being associated with queerness leads them to reject actions or behaviors that might be perceived as too soft. In Black culture, our aunties rarely referred to someone as gay or queer, instead opting to say that he had a little "sugar" in his tank or that he was a little sweet. A significant part of a masculine identity is constructed by trying to prove one's sense of heterosexuality (regardless of whether a person is actually heterosexual or not). It is the fear of queerness that drives men to sexualize women's bodies and to act out aggressively in an effort to prove that they aren't one of the "soft" or "sweet" ones. This dynamic is evident in the rituals of masculinity, where men engage in behaviors such as pretending to hit or intimidate each other to test their opponent's willingness to stand up for themselves or take it lying down.

So much of my shame around being perceived as soft is rooted in the way we discuss and perceive that quality, which has led myself, and many others, to believe that "soft" boys are not worthy of love and acceptance. Before anyone ever told me, I knew that I was a soft boy. As the author of this book, I'll admit that I still feel shame about this label, and that shame has sometimes led me to act in ways that are not authentic to who I am. Unlearning patriarchal masculinity is a lifelong journey with no clear end point, and as I continue on this journey, I've come to realize that there is a need for me to reclaim and embody the softness that I spent years rejecting.

I rejected this softness because I thought it was directly linked to my ability to fight or defend myself. But as I got into fights and won them, I realized that my softness wasn't about an inability to fight— it was about a desire not to.

When it became clear to others that I was a soft boy, some took it upon themselves to help transform me into a tough man. While it's easy to judge the older boys for these lessons, I believe it's important to acknowledge that from their perspective, they were teaching me how to survive. One of these survival lessons occurred when I engaged in a play-fight with one of my cousins who was around my age. Our older brothers had us do body shots—a timed fight where you can't hit each other in the face, just the body. I didn't want to participate in this play-fight, and there was nothing that motivated me to hit my cousin, but I felt compelled to prove that I wasn't soft. As the fight progressed, I took many hits and was losing terribly. There was nothing driving me to try to win. But as I started to feel the punches more, I remember getting frustrated and upset, which made me get my head in the game. I started to throw punches back and managed to block a few, too. At the end of the fight, I remember seeing a proud look on my brother's face. It wasn't about who had won or lost, but about proving that I could do it. This story didn't end with a victorious shout or a moment of glory. It ended with me crying. Not because of any physical pain, but because of how much I had hated that entire experience.

After that, I siloed my gentleness and softness so that I would never have to be put in a position to fight again or forced to prove how tough I was.

When we say that we want boys to be tough, we might assume that we're helping them to endure suffering and harsh environments without giving up. But what actually happens is we end up teaching boys to act violently when needed, to merely survive a difficult world. Toughness alone does not lead us to take a stand or to take action to change our circumstances—instead, that is the impact of courage. It is courage that moves us to speak out against injustice and thrive in the world, even when we are afraid or when there are risks attached to doing so. And I believe gentleness, not toughness, is what leads to true courage.

I like to think of gentleness as having a soft and tender heart toward humanity. Gentle people are compassionate, patient, kind, and empathetic. They often strive to listen to and understand the feelings and experiences of others. Gentleness makes us better partners, siblings, children, parents, and neighbors. By embracing gentleness, we create spaces that foster safety, empathy, and vulnerability. What I love about gentleness is that when it's lived out, it can lead us to be more courageous. In many ways, I think gentleness makes courage more obtainable.

If a person has a fear of public speaking, patriarchal courage would tell them that they just need to face their fears head-on, get over the anxiety, and go and do it. But when gentleness is applied, we would first affirm that their fear is valid and acknowledge how brave they are to be willing to confront their fear. From there, gentleness tells us to engage in small steps—practicing the speech alone, practicing it with others, and working our way up to the big moment. Gentle courage acknowledges that we are building a steady foundation and not just a facade of it.

You may feel like gentleness is "just not you," but my response to that is this: Is it that you're not gentle, or is it more so that you haven't allowed yourself to be? The first step in allowing myself to be gentle was reframing what I believed about my own softness. While I used to see my softness as a weakness or as something that made me less of a man, I now try to embrace the way it keeps me level-headed when engaged in conflict and how it helps me to humanize the people who make me upset. I love the way it makes me interact with my nieces and nephews and how it makes me truly want to know them and affirm them.

I embrace how it makes me a more compassionate leader and enables me to love.

DEVOTIONAL

A prime example of gentle leadership can be seen in Jesus. To truly grasp the radical nature of his leadership, we must examine current leadership practices, as well as those in the ancient Middle East. When leadership is influenced by patriarchy and White supremacy, it often takes on a colonial and dominating approach. This type of leadership focuses on exploitation and control, viewing people as profitable assets while neglecting their needs and well-being. Environments shaped by this leadership style are competitive, always striving for control, and quick to eliminate anyone who falls short of expectations (often ones that are hardly reachable anyway).

One of my favorite moments of Jesus's ministry is found in John 8:1–11. In this story, the Pharisees brought a woman caught in adultery and put her on full blast in front of Jesus and the entire community. There's so much to unpack in just this piece of the story. The obvious: well, what about the man? Even in the ancient world, men were able to dodge accountability when they had done wrong. There's also something to be said about the Pharisees' deep desire to see this woman not just held accountable but stoned to death.

Here, the Pharisees were displaying the very opposite of gentleness—they met this woman with harshness and roughness; I imagine they argued for "tough love," too. While the Pharisees approached this woman with great hostility, Jesus simply began to write on the ground with his finger (I imagine the Pharisees looked at him strangely). Then he got up and said, "He that is without sin among you, let him first cast a stone at her" (John 8:7, ASV). Jesus basically has the best "mic drop" moment. The Pharisees started to leave the scene one by one.

When it was only Jesus and the woman left, he asked her if anyone had condemned her or denounced her; her response was no. And get this, Jesus responded: "Neither do I condemn thee" (John 8:11, ASV).

Jesus did not meet the Pharisees' initial hostility with hostility. He remained calm. Men are often socialized to meet fire with fire. When someone says the wrong thing or looks in the wrong direction, we often feel an unwavering need to prove how tough we are by escalating the situation. If someone gets loud with us, in return, we get loud with that person. But Jesus didn't fall for the trap to escalate. He didn't rise up and try to fight the Pharisees. Instead, he made a statement that caused them to rethink their condemnation of this woman. In a moment where it could have been easy to publicly shame or humiliate her, Jesus addressed her with kindness. He didn't join the bandwagon of condemnation and judgment, but he humanized her and truly saw her, in a way that probably changed her life forever.

The Bible calls for Christians to embody gentleness, as the fruit of the Spirit is love, joy, peace, forbearance, kindness, goodness, faithfulness, gentleness, and self-control. I find it interesting to consider all the traits that do not feature on this list. The essence of the Spirit does not embody dominance, aggression, or violence. As the world, and particularly young people, continue to challenge societal norms around gender, there appears to be a movement within the church to reclaim "traditional" or "hegemonic" masculinity. However, this version of masculinity does not appear in Jesus's teachings, and it often leads us to a path of emptiness. But the embodiment of gentleness takes us on a path to living a more whole life.

Committing to embodying gentleness in everyday life will take some continued work to deconstruct the things that we believe about gentleness and masculinity. The "tough love" that was instilled in us may have taught us to be physically strong, but it did not teach our hearts to be strong to love. There's a beauty in softness that all humans deserve to experience. Whether it's through a soft and gentle touch or a voice, the spirit of gentleness will always push us to pause. To become more empathetic, thoughtful, and kind. Throughout this week, my challenge to you is to hug more, to kiss more, to pause before raising your voice, and to extend grace to yourself and to others.

PAUSE & REFLECT

In which areas of your life do you need to practice gentleness? What would embodying more gentleness in that area look like?

V

SILENCE

"My earliest memories are tainted by trauma, teaching me the painful lesson that masculinity means being unsafe. A boy, supposed to be a brotherly figure, sexually assaulted me throughout my childhood, distorting my understanding of healthy relationships and sex, even to this day.

Last year at a men's retreat, I had a moment when compassionate clarity bloomed within the fragmented pieces of myself: If I, a victim of sexual assault, felt too unsafe to speak out, who could this boy, likely equally terrified of his sexuality and mental illness, turn to?"

RON SPARKMAN

IMPACT CONFERENCE DECEMBER 2018

As Pastor Claudette Copeland delivered her sermon on secrets and sexual violence from 2 Samuel 13, a flood of childhood memories surged through me, evoking feelings of ambiguity and uncertainty that had lingered for years. These memories were rooted in games that lacked joy and were shrouded in a singular rule: "Don't tell anyone." They had carved a hidden chamber within me, their specifics blurry, but their lingering impact was felt in every corner of my life. During Pastor Copeland's message, the echoes of those memories persisted and radiated through my body.

When Pastor Copeland concluded her sermon, she invited the audience to stand. With a gentle yet compelling call, she reached out to those who had endured the darkness of sexual abuse or violence, asking them to meet her at the front of the conference hall.

At that precise moment, my heartbeat quickened and a wave of apprehension flooded through me, causing my hands to tremble—an automatic response that usually hinted at impending nerve-racking scenarios. I stood at an intersection, caught in the grip of a pivotal decision. Throughout her sermon, Pastor Copeland had talked about the tendency to shout over our pain by masking it with loud distractions—a truth that was so real for me. For years, I had been silencing my inner turmoil by burying myself in ceaseless activity, creating a safe distance from those who sought to truly know me.

I decided to step forward and meet Pastor Copeland at the front of the conference hall, ready to confront the secrets that had clouded over my heart.

With tears streaming down my face, I raised my hands in surrender, releasing my secret, shame, and guilt back to God. Emotions overwhelmed me, which was rare for someone who typically remained composed and calm in church. The weeping grew stronger, and I collapsed to my knees, trying to conceal my tears with one forearm while balancing on the other. Despite my attempts to hide my distress, my cries echoed throughout the room. It was the first time in a long time that I had cried without being under the influence of anything. There was a man singing on stage. Overwhelmed by my emotions, he released his mic, dashed off the stage, and rushed toward me, enveloping me in a tight embrace. I had never experienced such intimacy from another man. In that vulnerable instant, a stark contrast emerged between past childhood encounters with a male's touch and this present safe embrace from a different man, a stranger whose name I never learned, but whose touch changed my life forever.

What happened on this December day in Atlanta, Georgia, may seem strange to you, based on your experiences and history with faith or with the church. For some, this story may resemble the fearmongering and trauma-dump culture of nineties youth groups and church camps, or it may just seem like a bunch of emotionalism. Rather than intellectualizing or theologizing the experience, I take it for what it was—my experience. It truly marks an important moment in my healing journey. After what took place that day, I didn't walk around the building "healed" from my sexual traumas. I didn't become "free" from the weight of my childhood experiences. What did happen, though, was I became free from the chains of silence in relation to my experiences. It was a moment of truth-telling.

BREAKING THE SILENCE

A year later, I decided to go to therapy. I spent my first year in therapy talking about my sexual story—how I learned about sex, how I experienced it, and the memories I have of it. There were layers of shame that I needed to work through in order to walk the journey of healing. As I peeled back the layers, piece by piece, I was able to see how vulnerable I was in every story where I was harmed. Vulnerability almost became like a trigger for me as I internalized a false belief that it always leads to violation or demasculinization.

The common response to a survivor's story (regardless of their gender) is often, "Why didn't you say something? Why now?" My silence existed for many reasons. My perpetrators were both men and women, and none of them were strangers. We like to think of rapists or child predators as creepy old men who live alone in spooky houses, but not as our teachers, religious leaders, friends, or even family members. For a survivor to break their silence, they must expose themselves and another person—a choice that each survivor is entitled to handle with their own discretion.

Sexual assault[12] is something that anyone can experience, and often the shame experienced by men is related to the gender of the person who assaulted them. If the perpetrator is a woman, society doesn't always view it as assault (even though it is). The societal belief is that men should enjoy any sexual advances from a woman, which usually translates to a belief that women cannot actually assault a man. The porn industry, along with the media, has normalized a gross fantasy of underage boys sleeping with their adult teachers or their friend's

---

12. *Sexual assault*: Any form of sexual contact or action that happens without consent. This includes unwanted touching, forcing someone to perform oral sex, or penetrating someone's body.

mother, neglecting that consent cannot be granted when a person is underage. When these scenarios play out in real life, boys are often encouraged to see their assault as a badge of honor.

This changes drastically when the perpetrator is another man—in this scenario, male survivors often force themselves into an even deeper silence. There's the fear that people will question their sexuality, and the perception that they were too weak to "fight him off." One of the potential impacts of sexual assault is it can make a person question or be confused about their sexuality after being assaulted, regardless of the gender of the perpetrator. Yet, it is also important to understand that sexual assault is not related to the sexual orientation of the perpetrator or the survivor, and that one's sexual orientation is not caused by abuse or assault.

Not only did "the who" keep me silent, but so did my complex understanding of "the what." Trauma has the potential to impact your memory, giving your brain relief by trying to forget the difficult things. As years went on, I felt like I couldn't speak out because of the foggy nature of the details. What could I confidently say happened? I knew that what happened, happened, but I didn't want to admit it. Admitting it and breaking the silence would make it real. It would force me to wake up and realize that the nightmare was actually real life.

THE JOURNEY OF HEALING

When I reflect on what my healing journey has looked like, I can say it has consisted of a lot of therapy and many courageous conversations. While it's tempting to walk you through everything that I did and to give you all the details, I find it's important to acknowledge that even though our stories may echo with similarities, our journeys to healing may look different. However, I do want to leave you with three things that I think were important for me to know.

#1. *What happened to you, whether you were a child, teenager, or an adult, does not make you less of a man.*

For many men, our pride is something that gets in the way of addressing difficult things. Patriarchal masculinity teaches us that our manhood is defined by our ability to defend and protect others and ourselves. In addition to this, our pride tells us that we're supposed to just "get over it" and "move on" and not dwell on the past. But the only way to truly "move on" is to address it. I thought that not talking about it was making me stronger, when really it was making me weaker.

I'm sure many people, when they read this chapter, will commend me for my bravery. I acknowledge that what I'm doing is indeed brave, but it's something that's been easier to do because I've been talking about this more openly for a few years now. The more I talk about it, the less power it has over me.

#2. *The emotions you feel are valid, and you don't have to feel ashamed about showing them.*

Not showing sadness is not tapping into a human emotion that is essential for survival. The feeling of sadness is the way that our body communicates with us that something is wrong. When we don't tap into our sadness, it is easy for it to be replaced with other emotions, such as anger. Whichever way you feel is valid, and I encourage you to allow yourself to feel it all. The healing journey is full of multiple complex emotions, some that are often in conflict with others. Some days in therapy I felt rage; some days I felt peace.

#3 *What happened to you was not your fault.*

For many folks who were assaulted as children, it is easy to blame ourselves for our bodies' natural responses. Internally, we may say things like, "But I was hard," or, "I had an orgasm," and that must mean that it wasn't assault. It must mean that we wanted it to happen, and that we liked it. *No.* It is natural for your body to react in certain ways, and this was something that you did not have control over.

Patriarchy teaches men to "never back down" and to "fight to the finish," and maybe you also feel like you did not do that. You may reflect back on your experience and feel like there was more you could have done to resist, and maybe you blame yourself for not doing so. My friend, remind yourself that you did what seemed best at the time to survive—and there's nothing un-masculine about that.

SUPPORTING MALE SURVIVORS

Perhaps you're reading this book and you yourself may not be a survivor and feel distant from this chapter and context. While you may not know what it's like, I'm confident that you know someone in your life who has survived. If you're looking for ways to support them, here are a few.

The first thing you can do is listen and validate the feelings of a survivor. "I believe you," and, "That sounds like a really hard thing to go through," can go a long way. As you listen, remember to take yourself out of the center. Sometimes our natural reaction can be, "Who did it?!" "I swear I'll kill them right now!" That response isn't as helpful as it sounds. Part of taking yourself out of the center is acknowledging that you will also have feelings, but you were not the person assaulted. If you're a caretaker or a parent, you may want to express your guilt for feeling like you didn't protect them; but that is something that you have to work out separately, not necessarily with the survivor, at least not at the time when they first disclose what took place. Remember, it's not about you.

The best thing you can be for folks is a listening ear and a supportive and loving person, but you must know your limits. Don't try to be everything to that person—be what you can be and point to resources for what you cannot do, whether that resource is a support group, a book, or an article that can further support them.

A MESSAGE TO SURVIVORS

I wrote this chapter for the survivors out there. There may not be grandiose quotes or significant takeaways within these lines, but it was vital for me to create a space for those who comprehend this unique language and share similar experiences. This chapter is for those whose lives were forever altered by a single touch, those struggling to make sense of their trauma, and those like me—everyday individuals learning to live and heal.

To the men who are survivors: Know that you are not alone.

I believe you, even if specific details elude you or the full story remains buried in your subconscious. Trust yourself and believe your intuition, for often our bodies retain the true narrative better than our minds.

I'm sorry for the pain you've endured and the burdens you've carried in silence due to fear or shame. Please understand that it was not your fault, and owning your story—embracing it for yourself—is an act of bravery.

Should you ever feel overwhelmed by despair, or you are contemplating ending it all, please do not feel ashamed.

Your strength and resilience are undeniable, but there comes a time when even the strongest need support.

Your life holds immeasurable value, you are deserving of love, and your presence enriches this world in ways you may not yet realize.

You are cherished, you are valued, and you are never alone.

With love and solidarity,
Destyn Land

DEVOTIONAL

I struggled with the idea of writing a devotional for this chapter, grappling with the ways in which the church and religion have failed to support survivors and to hold religious leaders accountable for sexual violence. Religion has often been used to silence survivors, pressuring them to forgive without allowing space for mourning, and using "forgiveness" as a shield against accountability. We have sometimes created a false dichotomy between forgiveness and justice, implying they cannot coexist. Our stories of pain have been minimized as mere chapters in "God's plan," highlighting the murky territory religion enters when addressing sexual assault.

The topic of sexual assault and faith is complicated. In the Christian faith, we believe that God is omnipotent (infinite in power) and that God is close to the brokenhearted, intervening in their lives, and capable of preventing harm. This raises a challenging question that I have had to ask myself, and that many survivors grapple with:

Why didn't God stop it from happening?

As much as I wish I could, I know that this is a question I cannot answer. I don't know why God allows certain things, and it's okay for us to sit with that uncertainty. Sometimes, I think we feel obligated to speak for God in every instance as a means of defending His existence, or feel like if we cannot answer a question, we're punching holes in our faith. To question, to doubt is human. God is not afraid of your questions or your doubt.

While I may not be able to answer that question, here's what I do know:

God does not condone sexual assault or abuse.

God does not blame victims.

God is a God of Justice and will hold all of creation accountable.

I've found that when this topic comes up, the first tendency of the church is to theologize the experience. We try to hypothesize what God is saying or doing through our stories of abuse and harm, rather than answering the call to love and support those who have been abused. Romans 12:15 instructs us to "rejoice with those who rejoice; [and] mourn with those who mourn" (ASV). While the church excels at celebrating, we sometimes fall short in offering support during times of mourning.

Patriarchal masculinity teaches men to be independent and to rely on their own strength and capabilities. We can counter this by embracing interdependence and viewing our well-being, healing, and joy as interconnected, meaning that I cannot be well when my brother is unwell. I strive to understand my brother's sickness or despair deeply to a point where I am impacted, too. When we recognize the interconnectedness of our well-being, our communities will be compelled to be deeply affected and moved by the stories of survivors. If we approach their stories and pain as if they were our own, we would create environments conducive to the healing of survivors.

Neglecting to mourn with those who mourn is another form of minimizing their experiences. The mourning process enables us to collectively express our emotions (with the focus on the emotions of the affected individual), aids in coping, and is an essential aspect of the healing journey.

As questions continue to come up, and as you walk the messy path of healing, I hope you find comfort in knowing that God is with you in this very moment. Remember the words of Psalm 147:3: "[God] healeth the broken in heart, And bindeth up their wounds" (KJV).

PAUSE & REFLECT

What might "rejoice with those who rejoice; mourn with those who mourn" look like in action?

VI

ACCOUNTABILITY

"If love is a decision we make, accountability is the same. We have to decide to hold ourselves accountable and others accountable. If done with grace, accountability can truly be an extension and a manifestation of love.

I hear a lot of people talk about accountability, but often what they really mean is punishment."

SETH MCMANUS, INDIANAPOLIS, IN

FACEBOOK MESSENGER
9/16/21, 3:34 PM

Destyn: "I hate knowing the harm that I've caused and how that's impacted you. (Sorry if I'm over apologizing lol.) But man, I even have to apologize for the ways I thought of you that weren't positive. In the moment I didn't think that I was spreading a rumor. I thought I was just telling the truth. But that also neglects how easy it is to believe something when you've already thought thoughts that confirm what someone else says without addressing it with that person."

We exchanged Facebook messages back and forth, pouring out our feelings and confessing things we had kept hidden in person.

I had to face the truth that I had truly messed up.

For context, my friend and I had an extremely complicated relationship. As two Black men in the same program, at the same college, and living on the same floor of Urness Hall, we were constantly compared to each other, setting us up for unspoken competition. Being Black men at a predominantly White university meant we were often seen as both a risk and a token simultaneously. Globally, Black men have some of the lowest graduation rates, contributing to the perceived risk, which in turn leads institutions to tokenize us as the "good" Black men, holding us up as symbols of hope and progress. This complexity often manifested in our interactions—at our peaks we were closer than brothers, but at our lowest points we were each other's enemy.

The ideology of White supremacy insinuated that there was only room for one of us at the tables of power and privilege. While outwardly I rooted for him to claim that seat, deep down I wanted it for myself.

One day I heard a very vague rumor about him and chose not to seek clarification or ask follow-up questions; instead, I operated under confirmation bias. Having already harbored negative thoughts and beliefs about him, anything negative someone said only reaffirmed what I already believed to be true. When someone questioned me about him, I shared the rumor but filled in the gaps with my biases. It later transpired that my assumptions were wrong, but the damage was done—I had told one person who then spread it to many others, tarnishing my friend's reputation. We attempted to address the issue while still in school, but I wasn't prepared to take accountability; I persisted in deflecting blame onto him, focusing on his flaws and imperfections, even though they were irrelevant to the situation at hand.

Nearly two years post-graduation, I reached out to accept responsibility for my actions. This sparked a two-month-long conversation that ultimately led to forgiveness and reconciliation.

Reflecting on this chapter in my life, I am filled with overwhelming gratitude for my friend's grace and forgiveness, even though he had no obligation to do so. He had every right to cut ties with me, and I fully acknowledge that fact. Understanding this truth is crucial in grasping the complex and profound impact of grace and forgiveness. Its power becomes illuminated when we recognize that it is neither earned nor deserved, nor is it a mandatory response. No one is obligated to forgive us, nor are they obligated to welcome us back into their lives. It is a conscious choice.

And when that choice is made to extend forgiveness, it comes from a place of genuine compassion and love.

To my friend:

> *When you read this, thank you for granting me the messy and beautiful gift of grace, and thank you for being my friend.*
>
> *I love you.*

PAUSE & REFLECT

Can you recall a time when you made a mistake that had a negative impact on someone? How did you take accountability for your actions? If you didn't, how do you wish you had handled the situation differently?

ESCAPING ACCOUNTABILITY

The #MeToo movement has seen a number of spin-off initiatives aimed at holding individuals accountable for their actions, particularly in industries like the arts and music. In Minneapolis in 2020 a group of brave women decided to speak out against known sexual abusers in the arts and music industry by creating a platform for women to name their abusers. This aggregated list was made public to protect other women from potential harm caused by these individuals who may not have faced legal consequences.

As the movement expanded beyond the arts and music industry to include men in the Twin Cities at large, the list of names grew, with some becoming more recognizable. The response from the men whose names appeared on the list varied, with some choosing to remain silent on social media or deleting their accounts altogether. While this behavior by known perpetrators is absolutely not justified, it does raise questions in general about the challenges men face in taking accountability for their actions, especially when there are few examples of such accountable behavior from other men. This lack of visible accountability may contribute to the difficulty some men have in acknowledging and addressing their own wrongdoings.

Both accountability and forgiveness are vulnerable processes that uncover our rawest emotions. When we hold ourselves accountable, we uncover remorse, shame, and judgment. And when we choose to forgive, while it may lead to relief, the process usually involves grief, hurt, and disappointment. One of the greatest difficulties of engaging with the process of accountability is the way in which we navigate guilt and shame. When shame becomes a part of that story, we shift from feeling bad about what we've done to believing that we are bad for what we've done, and therefore don't deserve to be loved. As we've talked about before, shame calls us into hiding, and in terms of accountability, that hiding manifests as avoiding difficult conversations, blame-shifting, and moving on without acknowledging what took place.

Hiding can also be much easier for men due to the power and elevated standing that patriarchy has given them. Much of our perceptions of leaders involve a man or masculine characteristics. Men are more represented in organizational leadership within religious communities, schools, corporations, and government, creating an environment where it is easy for them to escape accountability. When this power is abused, it leads many to cover up their mistakes or pay their way out of accountability.

From Harvey Weinstein to R. Kelly and many other perpetrators, we often wonder how these men managed to escape accountability for so long. The answer is straightforward: Men are and have always been protected by patriarchy. The ability to hide becomes even easier if a man has done something to harm a woman, a population that patriarchy has deemed less than. When a society is shaped by the belief that men are superior to women, every system reflects this ideology, from government to education and beyond, which in turn contributes to the continued pervasive bias against women—a vicious cycle. In the legal system, officials often view women as liars or exaggerators, and they are skeptical of women who report abuse or harm, particularly if it comes from their partners. Men who commit violence against their female partners receive shorter sentences than those who commit violence against a stranger.[13] Additionally, judges have higher standards for what constitutes "evidence" of domestic violence or assault. Our society expects perfection from these women in order for them to be believed—and any perceived flaw or mistake they've made makes them "deserving" of their abuse. Under a patriarchal system, women and young people are left unprotected and vulnerable to exploitation and harm, as seen in the alarming rates of sexual violence and assaults on college campuses across the globe, where too often victims are blamed and perpetrators are unpunished.

Beyond the legal system, the social roles that we've designed for men and women, as well as for boys and girls, also dictate how we view and understand accountability. Based on these roles, we often don't even recognize male harm for what it is, and instead we always find a way to shift the blame back to the girl or woman. To illustrate this on a micro level, let me share with you an awkward, messy, and relatable middle school love triangle story.

When I was in seventh grade, I caught "the kissing disease," a.k.a. mononucleosis, and this became the biggest topic of discussion at school. The halls echoed with, "Who do you think he got it from?" and in the classrooms, theories were formed to solve the mystery.

---

13. Lundy Bancroft, *Why Does He Do That?: Inside the Minds of Angry and Controlling Men* (New York: Penguin, 2003).

After splitting with my eighth-grade girlfriend, I started dating and talking to a few different girls, all within the same friend circle (none of whom I actually kissed). The school community concluded the two most likely options of who I got mono from and subjected these young girls, who were the same age as me and likely also experiencing puberty, to slut-shaming. Behind closed doors, these young girls faced whispers about them being whores while nothing negative was said about me.

Later on in our adult life, I caught up with one of the women involved in the conflict. During our time together, we laughed about our middle school drama that felt like an episode of *Love & Hip-Hop*, but we also acknowledged the impact the conflict, which started with the kissing disease, had on her life. It had made her life drastically difficult and likely changed her forever. In that moment, she learned an important lesson about womanhood: Women will always be held to a different standard than men. They will be judged more harshly and blamed for what a man has or does not have.

One of the ways that we promote boys and men escaping accountability is by viewing mischief, disorder, and defiance as masculine characteristics. Self-control is an important human trait that is not often seen as a characteristic of masculinity. In my middle school love story, my classmates believed that I was kissing multiple girls at school. However, that wasn't the problem because that's what they believed I was "supposed' to be doing"—it was what our older brothers did, what perhaps some of our fathers did, and what was glorified in the media. As we have learned, society teaches boys and men that when it comes to sex and aggression, men "just can't control themselves." The phrase "boys will be boys" suggests that there is something natural about a boy's rough play or anger. The lack of self-control among men who embody patriarchal masculinity is a result of the fact that these men (often seen as "real men") will never back down. Whether it's sex, a challenge, a fight, or a round of drinks, to back down or yield is seen as a pivotal sign of weakness.

Societal beliefs regarding men and sex often revolve around the notion that men must have it, and that denying them sex is harmful. Epididymal hypertension (blue balls) is a condition that has been manipulated to coerce individuals into engaging in sex by suggesting it "hurts if they don't." This coercion even extends to the way we discuss sex with young people. When it comes to boys, "the talk" typically focuses on using protection and avoiding pregnancy, while for girls, it emphasizes the importance of virginity and the sanctity of their bodies. The major issue with how we address sex for all genders is the failure to emphasize that sex must begin with consent. Neglecting to stress consent leads many boys to believe that sex is their birthright, something they can have at any time and with anyone. Tragically, this has led to our current epidemic of sexual assault, caused by men who do not take accountability for their sexual desire, and promoted by a society that lets them get away with it and even applauds them for it.

PAUSE & REFLECT

Have you ever avoided accountability yourself or observed others doing so?

HOLDING YOURSELF ACCOUNTABLE

Guilt and shame are both complex emotions that arise after we've done something wrong. Throughout this book, we've discussed the negative impact of shame on our identity and self-worth, but we haven't explored guilt as much. Guilt emerges as an emotion when we've done, or perceived that we've done, some sort of harm. I often experience guilt as a heavy burden that I carry on my shoulders. When it arises, I try to examine it to distinguish it from shame. I analyze the thoughts in my head by asking myself, "Am I thinking about a specific thing I've done (guilt), or am I attacking who I am as a person (shame)? Am I thinking about how to repay or repair my wrongs (guilt), or am I thinking about how I can't be repaired or changed, and how I'm forever fragmented (shame)?" Sometimes, our thoughts can be a combination of both.

Paying attention to our guilt can be a valuable starting point for taking accountability. When I feel guilty about something, instead of ignoring it or trying to push it aside, I choose to delve into it with curiosity. I internally analyze what has transpired, my role in the situation, how it has affected someone else, and what I can do from there. Accountability is something we often demand from others, but we seldom discuss how to put it into practice. I don't claim to have all the answers on how to hold oneself accountable, but I can share how I personally approach it in my own life.

Taking accountability starts with confession: admitting what we've done and acknowledging the full extent of it. Avoid contextualizing what we did, making excuses, or minimizing it to appear smaller or less significant. My father used to talk about how when people make excuses for their actions, they often look to someone they perceive as worse than themselves to justify their shortcomings. With this mind-set, we tend to believe that as long as we are not engaging in the same behavior as our neighbor, friend, or brother, then we are in the clear. We use someone else's actions as a way to downplay our own. This minimization continues when we seek to justify why we acted as we did. We search for a way to prove that some external factor beyond our control inevitably led us to behave in this way.

For a long time, my childhood trauma was my excuse for every-thing. I weaponized my trauma and used it as a "get out of jail free" card. If I lied, I blamed it on my trauma. If I didn't text someone back, I blamed it on my trauma. This is not to say that our trauma doesn't play a role in shaping the way we act, but neither does it mean that our unaddressed traumas never lead us to do harm. The main point here is that trauma can often be a card that we play to excuse our actions. In doing this, we minimize the harm that others have experienced and center our own harm that they did not cause and are not responsible for.

We use our trauma to contextualize our behavior because we believe it makes us appear as less of a bad person. This is where understand-ing the difference between guilt and shame becomes important. When we experience shame after we've done something wrong, our typical response is to hide because shame targets our identity and says that we are undeserving. Hiding allows us to defend ourselves and our reputa-tion, but it distances us further from accountability. In comparison, guilt allows us to see that while our actions were wrong, they do not auto-matically mean we are a bad person. Instead, we are capable of change and making amends. This shift in mindset leads us to accountability.

After the confession comes acceptance. When we have harmed some-one, we don't get to tell them how they should feel, nor do we get to decide how they choose to pursue justice. When the lists of sexual abusers circulated in 2021, the men who did respond chose to emphasize how much they'd changed and transformed for the better, in the hopes of avoiding criminal charges. If we have committed a crime against someone, they have a right to press charges, and part of taking accountability is accepting the consequences of our actions. The consequences may include no longer having access to the person we have harmed, paying for any damage caused, or recognizing that we are not owed anyone's forgiveness.

Acceptance should be followed by commitment. Commitment might look different for everyone, and there is a lot of nuance based on the situation. For example, commitment can look like making amends, but sometimes the person you have wronged is not interested in having a relationship with you anymore. I personally see commitment as continuing to devote time and energy to personal growth. If your anger has led you to strike someone, it's commendable that you've confessed what you've done and accepted the consequences. The next step is committing to learning how to be better. This might involve taking a class, attending therapy, or simply taking time to reflect and process the events that took place.

HOLDING OUR FRIENDS, BROTHERS, AND HOMIES ACCOUNTABLE

While it is true that we can only be accountable for our own actions, we can also play a pivotal role in holding others accountable. One of the biggest obstacles that prevent us from doing this is a patriarchal loyalty to other men. Most definitions of *loyalty* involve a strong sense of support, devotion, or commitment to someone or something. This includes concepts such as faithfulness and love. However, patriarchal loyalty, often referred to as the "bro code," promotes a different approach. It teaches that men should prioritize their relationships with other men and turn away when their friends engage in harmful behaviors.

Historically, manhood was often linked to ownership, with a man's position on the masculinity hierarchy determined by what he owned. In the 1800s in America, this was based on White men's ownership of land and other humans (in other words, people who were *enslaved*). Today, a man's property is often considered his spouse and children. Interfering with a man's partner is seen as interfering with his property, which was historically associated with instigating violence. This broader message has led to the belief that reporting someone's actions, or "snitching," is a betrayal of the code that all men adhere to. Men who snitch are labeled as "bitches" and demoted from the status of a "real man" to a weaker, less powerful position—which, in a patriarchal society, is represented by women, considered the weakest and most vulnerable population.

The "bro code" is based on the belief that all of our male friends are inherently the "good guys," which can cause us to overlook their capacity to do harm out of a warped sense of loyalty. Even if we acknowledge that a brother has done harm, we often excuse his behavior because it fits into the socially accepted archetype of masculinity. Just because a friend or brother acts honorably and kindly toward you does not guarantee that they will always behave in this manner toward others, and just because his behavior is socially "acceptable" doesn't mean it is right. I used to believe that because I had never physically assaulted a woman, I was exempt from criticism and could pride myself on being a "good" man. However, I have engaged in laughter at sexist and misogynistic jokes that normalize violence against women and that perpetuate rape culture. When men choose to ignore their brothers' harmful actions or even affirm them for it, I believe this is the true betrayal that prevents us from being better.

Many men often wait until it is too late to hold their friends accountable. We wait for them to cross a line that we consider to be "too far." We wait for them to use force or commit the most extreme act imaginable. As long as they do not go too far, we are comfortable with their objectification of women, the way they pressure others into giving them their phone numbers, the way their comments make people feel uneasy, and so on. Holding our friends accountable means intervening sooner, even if it is to point out a certain word choice or microaggression that feels "harmless" (but isn't). It means being able to say, "Hey, what did you mean by that?" "Please don't say that because—" "What you did there was inappropriate and misogynistic."

Because our systems and institutions were designed to shield us from accountability, it is our responsibility as men to hold each other accountable and educate one another with love. If we don't, no one else will. Offering correction and accountability is a powerful way to say, "I love you," not only to the person being corrected, but also to the individuals who have been harmed by their actions. Our communities, families, and homes are strengthened by accountability and weakened by its absence.

PAUSE & REFLECT

Does "loyalty" ever contribute to your decision to remain silent? If so, when does this happen and why?

DEVOTIONAL

As a true Midwesterner, I must admit that I'm naturally inclined to avoid conflict. I dislike confronting people and often try to escape situations that might escalate. A misconception I had about conflict was that it always leads to rupture rather than repair. Through therapy, I learned that conflict can be an invitation to a deeper intimacy with the people we're in conflict with. However, from a patriarchal perspective, conflict often takes on an aggressive tone—or even becomes deadly. I've seen how engaging in conflict can lead men to physically fight or make threats against each other, which is something I'd rather not be a part of. A rule of patriarchal masculinity implies that if you're going to confront a man about his actions, you should be prepared to fight him.

In contrast, the biblical story of Prophet Nathan and King David offers an example of what it might look like to hold others accountable with compassion, love, and grace.

2 Samuel 11 tells a story about King David abusing his power and ultimately causing another man to be killed based on his own lust and selfishness. As the story goes, while walking on the roof of his palace, King David saw an attractive woman named Bathsheba bathing and took an interest in her. He sent someone to find out more information about her and learned that she was a married woman, the wife of Uriah, one of his soldiers. I think it's important to note that the abuse of power started before David found out that she was married; in fact, the story begins with abuse. Because David was a king, he acted as if his kingly title gave him the authority to look at a woman's naked body without her knowledge or consent. Knowing

that Bathsheba was the wife of one of his soldiers, I think David saw that he had an advantage—or a greater opportunity—to do what he wanted and not get caught (i.e., a way to escape accountability). King David sent his people to bring her to him. Bathsheba and David had sex, and Bathsheba became pregnant.

So far in this story, we see some interesting aspects of the society and culture at the time that relate to our own. As a king, David held a position of power and authority, which gave him a significant amount of freedom and privilege. This power dynamic is particularly concerning when it comes to his relationship with Bathsheba, as it would have been difficult for her to say no to his advances, even if she had wanted to. We can't know for certain whether the sexual encounter between David and Bathsheba was consensual or not, but it's clear that David's kingly status would have created a significant power imbalance, making it difficult for Bathsheba to exercise agency or consent.

Faced with an unexpected child, David responded with shame in a way that is very familiar: He attempted to hide and cover up what had taken place by relieving Uriah of his soldier duties and sending him home to have sex with Bathsheba. But Uriah was disciplined and loyal to his job duties. His fellow soldiers were still at war, and it didn't sit well with him to abandon them. When the initial plan didn't work, David figured that if he could get Uriah drunk enough, he would go home and sleep with his wife, but that didn't work either. When all else failed, David sent Uriah to the front lines of the war without any backup or support, ensuring that he would be killed.

After sleeping with Bathsheba, David had many opportunities to hold himself accountable for the wrong he had done. But in his pursuit of covering it up and keeping his hands clean, he killed a man—something that was never part of the initial plan. This is an important lesson: Not owning up to our mistakes or dodging accountability always leads to us doing more damage and harm. David eventually took Bathsheba as his wife in an attempt to rebrand himself as the hero of this story, saving the poor pregnant woman of one of his captains through the institution of marriage to show his commitment to care for her for life.

It seemed like David was going to get away with it all, but God would not allow that to happen. Nathan, in the spirit of gentleness, approached David and told him a parable about two men, one poor and one rich. The rich man owned many sheep and cattle, but the poor man only had one ewe lamb—a female lamb that he cherished almost like a daughter. When a traveler entered the town and was welcomed by a feast, the rich man decided to kill the poor man's ewe lamb rather than take one of his many that he did not have a close relationship with.

Upon hearing this story, David became upset and demanded that the rich man be killed as punishment for what he did to the poor man.

Nathan responded, "Thou art the man!" (2 Samuel 12:7, KJV).

After Nathan told this story, David took accountability by confessing and acknowledging what he had done, and accepting God's consequences for his actions.

This story beautifully depicts the way we can hold those close to us accountable. Because of Nathan's role as both a prophet and adviser, he had to say something to the king. It would almost be unethical if he hadn't. Often, we see holding someone accountable as shouting at them, shaming them, or sometimes even using physical violence as a way to "teach them a lesson." Patriarchal accountability has a mob mentality and is about repaying blood with blood. However, Nathan was gentle and direct. He came to David with a story that awakened his guilt and led to his repentance.

In this journey of life, we all need Nathans—and sometimes we need to be Nathan—to find the courage to, as Malcolm X said, stand up for justice and truth "no matter who it is for or against."[14]

PAUSE & REFLECT

Have you ever found yourself in a situation where you needed someone to hold you accountable for your actions, or where you had to hold someone else accountable in a gentle and effective way? How did that experience impact you and your relationships?

14. Malcolm X and Alex Haley, *The Autobiography of Malcolm X* (New York: Ballantine Books, 1973).

VII

BROTHERHOOD

"At age sixty-three, God has blessed me with a diverse group of men who transcend age, culture, education, faith, income, politics, and sexuality. Their loving acceptance fosters a spirit of care, intimacy, and trust I have never experienced. Our brotherhood entails disappointment, empathy, fear, insecurity, joy, loss, and safety. We express our painful truths, honor our ancestral brilliance, respect our stated boundaries, and ultimately laugh at the insanity of the choices we make.

I feel more connected emotionally to my friends than my three brothers, which hurts my heart because the affection I longed for was never realized in my youth."

MARK TUGGLE, NEW YORK CITY, NY

"IT'S ALL GOOD"

never thought that Bobby, a Hmong American man who grew up in the suburbs, and whom I had initially shared no common interests with, would still be my friend today and the best man at my wedding.

Our friendship was consistent, but it was certainly rocky at times, and our fear of vulnerability exacerbated the rockiness. When we were in conflict with each other, rather than opening up and talking about how we felt, we would always downplay our conflict. Our masculinity rule books taught us that men don't get their feelings hurt, especially not by other men. In response to these rules, we would say things to each other like, "It's not that big of a deal," or, "It's all good," as a way of attempting to minimize the impact of the conflict. The downplaying and dodging continued through our denial of the conflict's existence and our interactions, as if everything were okay between us. In our worst conflicts, we would completely distance ourselves from each other and use silence as a weapon.

These habits were all forms of stoicism that we used to mask our hurt and attempt to cover up the elephant in our dorm room. The art of stoicism was an art form that masculinity taught us a long time ago, and one that every boy learns at some point in their life. We, like many other men, became stoic because we believed that if we didn't show that we cared, it would make dealing with hurt or rejection easier. This is one of the reasons why, throughout my life, I have often downplayed my excitement for something, whether it's a new job or a new opportunity, believing that not getting my hopes up will make dealing with the despair of disappointment easier. Engaging in this practice for some time now has taught me that stoicism doesn't make the bad feelings go away; instead it usually has the opposite effect—it made my highs lower and dampened the moments of celebration for any success.

The most unfortunate part of stoicism, and the rejection of vulnerability, is how it pushes us further and further away from the people we love and desire to be close to. As Bobby and I grew from boys to men, we made the choice to drift apart from each other rather than confront the conflict that had developed between us.

This changed drastically the night we almost got into a fight.

That day, our tensions had boiled over into a heated argument, with harsh and hurtful words exchanged. This was our moment, at least the way we saw it at the time, to expose each other's flaws. As former roommates for three consecutive years, we knew things that others didn't—that our stories and images weren't as squeaky-clean as those around us perceived. As emotions escalated, my impulse to fight emerged, a learned response from my school environments where conflicts were often settled through physical confrontation. In the hood if you couldn't resolve the conflict, you had to "fight it out."

"So, you wanna fight me?" I yelled into the phone, hastily putting on my shoes and making my way to Bobby's apartment. Locked in a physical struggle, we pushed and screamed at each other, both anticipating a potentially violent outcome. Bobby didn't actually want to fight me, but he relented because he thought it was what I wanted and needed. Grappling with my own power struggles, I knew fighting Bobby would not bring any resolution. Yet, as uncomfortable as it is to admit, at that moment I believed that throwing a punch would make me more of a man. I convinced myself that I was standing my ground and sticking up for myself.

In reality, I was living behind the mask, possessed by the rules we live by, and using violence as a shield to hide my own hurt.

At the crescendo of our clash, Bobby's voice shattered the tension as he told me he loved me. The three words he spoke had a sobering effect on both of us, awakening us to the reality of the situation.

You love me? I thought to myself. Something about those words made all the anger inside of me dissipate. We both cried the tears we'd held in for years and hugged each other as if we never wanted to let go.

Shortly after our outburst, Bobby lit a cigarette as we took a long walk, aimlessly wandering through the city. Finally, we were able to say the words to each other that still keep us close today:

"I'm sorry."

The tale of Bobby and me is a story about how the avoidance of vulnerability among friends and brothers often leads to resentment. If we don't address our feelings, especially when they are hurt, we allow them to grow and sprout into contempt for those whom we love.

PAUSE & REFLECT

Think about a time you had a conflict with a close friend or a brother. What emotions did you feel, and how did you deal with the conflict?

ARE YOU YOUR BROTHER'S KEEPER?

The way we handle conflict, communicate our emotions, and confront vulnerability are all shaped by our beliefs about masculinity, which in turn significantly impact how we form and nurture connections with others.

For many men, including myself, our relationships with other men we consider friends or brothers can be complex and multifaceted, often oscillating between closeness and distance. This closeness is often defined by what we are willing to do *for* these men, but not by what we're willing to endure *with* them. For instance, many men would sacrifice their own lives for their brother, but they wouldn't feel comfortable showing empathy by holding him during a moment of vulnerability. While they would give their last breath for their brother, they would not extend that same level of trust and intimacy by being vulnerable themselves.

Many of us were taught to be "our brother's keeper," which, through a patriarchal lens, is often interpreted as providing tangible support and resources (money, shelter, etc.). Addressing the tangible needs of our brothers is important, but it's not the way to build connection. Bonds aren't solely formed by what we provide but are formed by how we show up and are present with one another. It's not just about the actions we take but about the emotional intimacy and vulnerability we're willing to share.

We often see vulnerability as being open and therefore susceptible to harm, which can be uncomfortable and even daunting. I like to think of it as the discomfort of being naked in a room of strangers. Our physical bodies are natural and familiar to us, but we typically cover them with clothes as we go about our day. When we remove our clothes, others can see intimate parts of us that they may judge or criticize. Similarly, our inner thoughts, struggles, and true selves are usually hidden behind an emotional armor we've built around ourselves, protecting them from being seen by others. This armor serves as a natural defense mechanism, allowing us to safeguard our vulnerability and imperfections. When we shed this armor and let our authentic selves shine through, we risk being seen and accepted for who we truly are—flaws and all.

It's important to acknowledge that vulnerability is hard for

everyone, and anytime a person sits in its discomfort, they are showing an act of bravery and courage. There is a need for us to humanize our collective struggle with vulnerability as we acknowledge how
the rules of masculinity hinder our ability to be brave and courageous through its displays.

In bell hooks's book *A Will to Change*, she notes that "when culture is based on a dominator model, not only will it be violent, but
it will frame all relationships as power struggles."[15] This notion of
dominance perpetuates a culture where we view others, particularly
men, as competitors in a relentless competition for wealth, status, and
power. As a result, we are conditioned to constantly size each other
up, comparing our abilities and achievements. When we first meet
someone, we often ask questions about their work or career to gauge
who might have a higher job title or salary. We bring up controver-
sial topics to test intellect and determine who's smarter. We examine
their bodies, looking for signs of physical strength, and imagine who
could win in a fight. We interact as if we're conducting a never-ending assessment to determine who the most powerful man is.

The constant sizing up that occurs in a culture of competition
hinders our ability to be vulnerable. When we're constantly evaluating each other's strengths and weaknesses, our vulnerabilities become
ammunition for teasing or shaming. I witnessed this firsthand while
working in a program for Black college men. During group check-ins,
students would often lie about their academic struggles, but when
they were alone with me in my office, they would openly discuss
specific classes or professors that were challenging them. They were

---

15. bell hooks, *The Will to Change: Men, Masculinity, and Love* (New York: Simon & Schuster, 2003).

afraid to share their struggles with their peers because they feared that they would become the subject of their jokes. I often wanted to tell my students that they should go talk to one of their peers, knowing that this person was struggling with the exact same class as them. If they could have moved beyond their competitiveness to reveal their vulnerabilities, they would have been able to support each other to aid in everyone's success.

When our relationships are built on competition, we can't truly be our brother's keeper because the individual's interests will always take precedence over the collective's well-being.

PAUSE & REFLECT

What societal pressures, personal biases, or past experiences have made it difficult for you to be vulnerable and to open up with your emotions?

FROM COMPETITION TO COMPASSION

One way we overcome our collective struggle with vulnerability is by unlearning the patriarchal rule that men should be self-reliant and replacing it with a new rule that encourages men to be compassionate. The word *compassion* means "to suffer together," and when we suffer together, we drastically change our approach to friendship and brotherhood.

Competition and self-reliance often go hand in hand, leading individuals to prioritize their own growth and progress over seeking help from others. When we approach life through a competitive lens, our individual achievements become the sole measure of success, making it difficult to ask for assistance, especially from other men who, based on the rule book, are our rivals. For a long time, I believed that it was my independence—my ability to pick myself up by the bootstraps to do things by myself—that made me a man. Because of this belief, I, along with many other men, would have rather risked breaking or damaging a brand-new piece of furniture in the process of putting it together rather than simply asking someone for help. To combat this, I have transitioned from viewing help as a sign of need to seeing it as an opportunity for community and connection.

Help may not be required to complete a task, but it can make the task more innovative, fun, and efficient. Compassion, in many ways, involves making a conscious decision to live life with others, recognizing that life is richer and more meaningful when shared side by side and face to face.

The thing is the friendships and connections that many men form are often created in a parallel manner, where they are never actually facing each other. In most of my relationships with other men, there's usually something that we're gathering to do—to play video games, go bowling, or watch a sports game together—but we don't always gather simply because we want to see each other. My relationships with my women or gender nonconforming friends are vastly different and always have a face-to-face element. We regularly call each other just to talk, to vent about something that happened during the day, or to sit with our feelings over life's many stressors. We're more likely to catch up over coffee, dinner, or a casual outing. We don't need a specific reason or purpose to connect—we gather because we've determined that we're going through life together.

While the face-to-face approach is often associated with feminine practices, it's crucial that we shift this perspective to recognize it as a fundamental human need. All of us need relationships that encompass both face-to-face and side-by-side interactions, as doing life in this way allows us to be seen, known, and understood in all dimensions of our lives.

When we suffer together, we start to desensitize ourselves to the discomfort that comes with vulnerability, to the point where it becomes a daily practice. Compassion requires us to do life not at a distance but up close and intimately, being present with each other whether we are better or worse, richer or poorer, and in sickness and in health. While romantic partnerships and friendships are different, they undoubtedly have some similarities. The vows that we take when getting married are similar commitments that we make to friends and brothers whom we love. These commitments are centered around being present for each other, which always has a way of helping us to see that we're not alone.

As we cultivate this kind of compassionate presence in our relationships, we also create an environment that invites accountability to thrive, allowing us to support each other through life's challenges and setbacks. In these face-to-face relationships, when our brothers or friends make mistakes, we are less likely to abandon them and will walk with them instead. We can support them through compassion and at the same time gently hold them accountable for their behavior by connecting them to resources, encouraging them to seek help, and pushing them to see the impact of their actions. When we do this, our shame cannot thrive because both silence and judgment are removed.

While it may be daunting to shun the protective mask we wear in order to embrace vulnerability and compassion, the ultimate pay-off far outweighs the initial discomfort—a deep sense of connection with both oneself and those around us.

DEVOTIONAL

In the Bible, the concept of brotherhood makes its first appearance alongside the world's first recorded murder.

The story of Cain and Abel, the earliest siblings in the Bible, illustrates this point. According to Genesis 4:4, Abel, the younger sibling, offered a sacrifice to God, presenting "the firstlings of his flock and of the fat thereof" (ASV). God was pleased with Abel's offering. In contrast, Cain's sacrifice did not receive the same favorable response from God. This seeming indifference on God's part enraged Cain, who became consumed by jealousy and eventually decided to take his brother's life.

What always strikes me about this story is the recognition that no one had ever been murdered until two siblings, Cain and Abel, entered the world and began to fight for dominance—something that men today are still fighting and dying over. Whether it's global wars or the local violence that feels like a war in our communities, much of it exists because of men's inability to talk through their problems or rein in their thirst for competition. From the ancient world to today, men have used violence to deal with their frustration. I imagine what frustrated Cain the most about God being more pleased with his younger brother than him was what it might have suggested about his masculinity or his view of himself. Cain probably believed, as the older brother, that he was supposed to be stronger and better than Abel, and he was prompted by competition and fueled by a sense of rivalry.

If Cain had been able to shift from competition to compassion, he would have been able to get curious about Abel's sacrifice without comparing it to his own self-worth. He would have asked more genuinely, "What was it about Abel's sacrifice that God was pleased with, and how might I learn from it?" I think we all face moments in our lives where we see or meet someone who does the thing we're good at better than us, and we start to act just like Cain. While this feeling has never led me to physically kill anyone, I have seen it lead me to find every reason to discredit another person's ability and diminish their character—all because of jealousy, competition, and the scarcity mindset that comes with it.

The story of Cain and Abel offers a poignant reminder of how the seeds of competition can sprout into trees of envy, burnout, and even violence.

The Bible also shows that brotherhood and relationships among men don't have to look this way. In Mark 9, while everyone gathered for dinner, Jesus got up and decided to wash all of his disciples' feet to set an example of how they must interact with one another. In the ancient world, foot-washing was a requirement before entering someone's home. As people mostly wore sandals and walked long distances, you can only imagine the dirt and sweat that stuck to their feet. The job of foot-washing was typically the task of a servant or a slave. For Jesus, their Lord and Rabbi, to wash all of their feet was to level out the power imbalance and resist the culture of competition.

In the Gospels of Matthew, Mark, and Luke, another story is told about the disciples arguing about who was the greatest or most superior of the twelve—a familiar tendency we exhibit when we're in a group of great men, whether it's rappers or athletes, businessmen or politicians. Rather than acknowledging all the strengths each person brings to the table, we seek to identify who is the greatest of all time.

In the Gospel according to Mark, Jesus responded to this debate and argument by saying, "If any man would be first, he shall be last of all, and servant of all" (Mark 9:35, ASV).

In this scripture, Jesus taught his disciples a valuable lesson that remains relevant today. His words offered a reminder that the pursuit of success often comes at the expense of others, as we cut corners and compromise our values in our quest to get ahead. When we choose to be humble and prioritize the collective good, we move through the world with a sense of unity and purpose. The irony of Jesus's teaching is that our desire to be first and foremost can actually obscure us to the reality that, in the end, everyone is deserving of ultimately reaching their goals.

When we view life through the lens of compassion, we realize that there are enough resources to go around, not just for some but for all of us.

PAUSE & REFLECT

What are the ways in which you often respond to feelings of competition or jealousy, and how can you shift from competition to compassion in those moments?

VIII

FATHERHOOD

"Growing up without my father, I have been fathered by many men throughout my life. This has shaped my conception of fatherhood into a kaleidoscope of philosophies about manhood. While I am fortunate to have diverse perspectives on what it means to be a man, it can be confusing to navigate without a single, definitive vision of masculinity.

The silver lining is that I get to choose what fatherhood means for myself. The myth of fatherhood suggests it must conform to a singular model, but in reality, if we're lucky, we have many fathers. Even more valuable than luck is the ability to define."

BOBBY CHAN YANG, MINNEAPOLIS, MN

THE HANDSHAKE

As I finished packing up my bedroom, it was almost eerie how empty and lifeless it looked. The walls, once covered with memories and posters, now stood bare. The usual chaos of a typical teenager's room was strangely calm. This room had been my only home and my only sanctuary, and now I was about to leave it to attend college. Just as I was about to go, my father knocked on the door and entered quietly. With a soft smile, he extended his hand to me and said, "Destyn, it was really nice having you here." In those simple words, I felt his sense of pride in who I'd become, his sadness at seeing me go, and his happiness at watching me embark on a new chapter in my life.

This handshake is a memory that I'll never forget.

In my earlier explorations of masculinity, I carried a lot of anger and did not have much grace for anyone else. I believed that everyone should live out their masculinity the way that *I* thought they should. Eventually, I learned that there was nothing liberating or radical about that. To suggest that there's only one right way to be masculine—even if that masculinity is healthy—is just as harmful as the embodiment of patriarchal masculinity. We can't be liberated from one box just to put ourselves in a different one.

There were times when I thought of this handshake and saw my dad's actions as a clear example of toxic masculinity. I thought to myself, *Your son is leaving. Kiss him on his forehead and tell him you love him so much. Squeeze him tightly, give him one of those hugs that suggest you never want to let him go. Look at him the way your eyes joyfully met his eyes the day he was born, when his tears never sounded like noise but like the gift of life.* I wanted to experience my father's touch and warmth.

My internal dialogue didn't leave much space for the fact that people show love the best way they know how. Sometimes, it isn't exactly what we want, but it does not represent the absence of love. When we don't get what we need or want, we may become dedicated to giving others what we didn't have. But if we give from a place of bitterness or hurt, every time we give, it's not actually about who we're giving to but rather about us. The reality is that what some may need and want can be entirely different from what we ourselves desired. While I was a kid who really loved and needed a lot of physical touch to feel affirmed and safe, I've met many young people and adults who have no interest in being embraced frequently in this way.

As someone who tends to seek out meaning in everything, I admit that I often try to find and create meaning in my experiences. As I matured, I began to realize that this handshake held a deeper significance than what I had originally thought. My father's handshake symbolized honor and respect. He had been brought up in a time when a handshake carried more weight than a signature. For him, the handshake represented my transition from boyhood to manhood, as well as the transition of his physical protection of me to a solely spiritual one. Through his handshake, he was acknowledging that it was my time to navigate life, discover my true self, and make my own decisions. It symbolized a transfer of trust, signifying that my dad had been a reliable father, and now it was my turn to venture out and become a respectable man. Initially, I had viewed that handshake as insignificant, but now I cherish it as one of my fondest memories with him.

PAUSE & REFLECT

How did your father or masculine parental figure express affection toward you? How would you describe the impact of their affection on you?

TOUGH LOVE

The goal of both fatherhood and brotherhood is to help boys become men. Walking through my own complexities with my father has taught me that the relationships fathers have with their sons, uncles with their nephews, and big brothers with their little brothers play a huge role in one's identity formation. The lessons of masculinity that have stuck with me the most are the ones that have come from my father—specifically, his belief that manhood is about responsibility and integrity. He made sure that all of his children had jobs as early as they could work because he wanted to ensure that we learned the importance of managing our money and living within our means. Without a doubt, there were other implicit lessons I learned from him, too.

One of our favorite childhood activities was going to Blockbuster to rent movies, and for a long time it was very predictable what movies I was going to rent—anything with Mary-Kate and Ashley Olsen in it! I loved the teen coming-of-age stories or really anything that would have been deemed a "chick flick." Although I didn't share similar identities with the characters in those shows, something about their experiences resonated with me. What I loved most about the "girly" shows was the plot—there was always a boy who met a girl, and even if they were too young to fall in love, they wallowed in the ambiguity of teenage infatuation. As a boy, I was very in touch with my feelings and was always looking for movies that could make me feel. But I think this was complicated for my dad. On one hand, he probably knew that these were just movies and that there wasn't anything inherently bad about them; on the other hand, he believed that these kinds of movies weren't "boy" movies, and if I didn't start liking those movies, how would I ever become a man?

To ensure that we were renting age-appropriate movies, we would always have to show our dad what we wanted to rent so that he could approve them. I imagine that he was also screening for gender-appropriate movies. To help me become a "man," in my father's eyes, he began to place a limitation on the number of Mary-Kate and Ashley Olsen movies I could rent. Slowly and gently, my dad started asking me to find different movies and different stories. Eventually, I traded in the Olsen twins for Power Rangers and Teenage Mutant Ninja Turtles—both shows about heroes who fight against villains, symbolizing the belief that "real men" had to fight bad men to save women and children, the most vulnerable in our communities.

Boys are raised with "tough love" because war is what the world will always expect of them. In Black fatherhood, there is a different approach to tough love. Black fathers often raise their sons with tough love because they know that grace will not be extended to them in society. During adolescence, Black boys are perceived as being three to four years older than they are. When they are ten years old, their teachers treat them like they are thirteen, and when they are fourteen or fifteen, the criminal justice system and schools seek to hold them accountable as adults. When I was a kid, I had a slight stealing problem. Whether it was at school or in someone's home, I was finding small things to take that were not my own, and I always managed to get caught. My dad wasn't a very aggressive man who physically disciplined us frequently, but the last time I stole, he disciplined me—and disciplined me good. In the lecture before the whooping, I'm sure he gave a variation of the infamous "it hurts me more than it hurts you" speech, but most importantly, he let me know that if I continued to do this later in life, the consequences would far exceed any short-lived pain of this spanking.

When I first entered the working world, I struggled with how White it was and how there seemed to be little interest in talking about how racism and patriarchy intersect. While patriarchy allows men to dodge accountability, when it intersects with racism, it specifically allows White men to dodge accountability and is constantly looking for a way to hold a Black man accountable, particularly in the criminal justice system.

When Black fathers raise their sons, I wonder if there is almost a fear that if they love them too affectionately or if they are too gentle with them, their sons will grow up unprepared for a world that doesn't love them.

PAUSE & REFLECT

What lessons about manhood did your father or another masculine adult figure teach you? How do these lessons shape the way you live out your masculinity now?

AFFECTIONATE FATHERHOOD

What a father believes about masculinity impacts the way they raise their children of all genders. Through the process of parenting, children learn most of the rules of the masculinity rule book. For fathers, this rule book is almost like a family heirloom that was passed down to them from their own father, and from their father's father, and so on. Similar to many traditions and legacies, these rules sometimes become outdated, or the context in which they were created no longer applies, but we continue to pass these values on because it is all we know.

I would argue that one of the things humanity could benefit from is a more affectionate fatherhood. In our pursuit of raising tough and strong boys, we deny them love as if it's something that they age out of. This denial leaves many boys deprived of touch, and all forms of physical affection become associated with sex. Some young men may constantly seek quick hookups because of their deep desire for affection.

Fathers who embody patriarchal masculinity can often seem emotionless. They never show or tell you how they are actually doing, and when they encounter rough patches, they isolate themselves from their families. I believe that there is a need for fathers, and ultimately men in general, to hug more, kiss more, and touch more. However, I think this goes beyond just physical affection—it's a call for men to love, and to love actively. Loving actively as a father involves emotional support, communication, understanding, and being present for their children and loved ones. It's about showing love in all aspects of life, not just through physical touch.

My father was never the most physically affectionate with his sons after they reached a certain age, but he never once stopped showing us that he loved us. His affection may not have been physical, but he still shows it every time he calls me. My dad will call me at least once a week if not every day, sometimes to ask a question or to get computer help. But really, he calls just to hear me breathe.

He calls just to hear my voice—not usually wanting anything but to know that I'm still living and I'm still his.

I love you, Dad.

PAUSE & REFLECT

How have you experienced affection from men in your life, and how might you show more affection to a boy or man in your life?

DEVOTIONAL

One of my favorite stories in the Bible, and probably one of the most well-known, is the Parable of the Prodigal Son.

Everyone, including the Pharisees, scribes, tax collectors, and those deemed sinners, approached Jesus to listen as he began to tell the story of a lost son. There were two sons born to a wealthy family. When the younger of the two asked his father if he could have his inheritance early, his father agreed. In a few days, the younger son took all of his belongings, left his father's home without mentioning his departure, and went to another country where he quickly blew all of his inheritance.

While we don't know specifically what the son used the money on, the Bible says it was all spent on "foolish living" (Luke 15:13, ASV). If this parable were told today, it might have included spending on gambling, drugs, and alcohol—or even simple things like eating out every day or expensive clothes. When the place where the son had gone to experienced severe famine, he had nothing left. The famine was so severe and the son was so broke that he had to work in the field to feed pigs. He couldn't even afford to eat what the pigs were eating.

Then, the son had an "aha" moment when he realized that he shouldn't have left his father's house in the first place. He remembered that his father always had enough for him to eat. Feeling remorseful and ashamed of his actions, he made the decision to journey back home to his father.

The son assumed that when his father heard about what he had done, he would be rejected. Because of this fear, he prepared a speech to give to his father when they met face-to-face. In this theoretical speech, he planned to confess what he had done with the inheritance, acknowledging that he didn't deserve to still be called his father's son and offering to serve as one of his father's servants. The son likely practiced this speech countless times while making the journey back home, but he never got the chance to say it.

Although the son was still a long way away, his father saw him in the distance. When he realized it was his son, the father began running toward him. He didn't make his son walk the whole way but instead met him where he was. This father didn't use the distance as a way to give his son "tough love" or to teach him a lesson. When he reached his son, he embraced him by "throwing his arms around him and kissing him" (Luke 15:20, NIV).[16]

The compassion that the father had for his son didn't stop there—he then clothed his son in a robe and ring and threw him a welcome-home party.

When we dive deeper into the context in which this parable was written, we observe a new significance in the father's actions of running toward his son. In that era, it was uncommon for men to run. Men often wore tunics that they would have to lift up if they decided to run—the problem was that lifting up their tunics would reveal their bare legs, which was considered extremely shameful at that time.

When the father decided to run toward his son, he took on the shame that his son felt. Can you imagine what the son looked like as he entered their village? He was a privileged kid returning to his home looking worse than a servant. As he got closer, I imagine he was spotted by others in the community who probably looked at him

---

16. *Bible, New International Version* (London: Hodder & Stoughton, 2007).

with judgment. Some probably laughed at him, while others were embarrassed for him. But the father refused to let his son face the crowd alone and didn't care if that meant bringing shame or dishonor to himself. Showing his son affection was more important to him.

When we examine this parable through a lens of fatherhood, we see a father willing to break the rule book of masculinity set by his culture to welcome his son back home. For the son, this kind of love was transformative, in the same way that God's love is transformative for us.

I think it's important to mention that fathers don't have to wait for their children to become prodigals before they love them like one. If you look for it, there is a daily opportunity to show young people the same kind of compassion, grace, and love that the father showed his son in this parable.

When we uncover the mask of masculinity, we will find beauty and love underneath. When the love that we give is filtered through patriarchy, it isn't actually love.

1 Corinthians 13:4–8 reminds us:

> "Love is patient, love is kind. It does not envy, it does not boast, it is not proud.
>
> It does not dishonor others, it is not self-seeking, it is not easily angered, it keeps no record of wrongs. Love does not delight in evil but rejoices with the truth.
>
> It always protects, always trusts, always hopes, always perseveres.
>
> Love never fails" (NIV).[17]

---

17. *Bible, New International Version* (London: Hodder & Stoughton, 2007).

PAUSE & REFLECT

In what ways do you feel called to break the rules to show love to yourself, your neighbor, and your community?

IX

LOVE

"Love means that I allow myself to be fully known and cared for by another. It means that I am committed to someone or something because they deserve it. It means allowing myself to be vulnerable with another, so that we can journey together.

As a man who also roots my identity in queerness, I have had to break through masculine stereotypes so that I can fully allow myself to be loved and to love others through my innate being."

CODY SUGAI, SEATTLE, WA

*SPOILER ALERT: THIS DREAM COMES TRUE (MAY 31, 2024)

Some boys dream of becoming a doctor, buying their dream car, or playing on a professional sports team. As for myself, I dreamed of meeting her, wondering how old I would be and where I would find her. I made up stories that reflected teen movies, and when I finally found her, I discovered something better than anything and everything I had ever dreamed of.

In fifteen days as of this writing, I will say the words I've dreamed of saying—*I do.*

Before we got engaged, people would often ask me, "Do you think she's the one?" I had been asked that question anytime I dated someone, and I had been wrong too many times to trust my answer. So, I decided to start asking myself a new question: "What if Netta isn't the one?" This question always made my stomach turn a little bit. I didn't ask it just on our best days but also on our toughest days—the days we argued or the days our differences seemed insurmountable. Asking this question felt strange, because for every dream I had about my future, she was a part of it. For every goal I had or for everything I hoped to accomplish, I wanted her to do it with me.

When I asked myself, "What if she isn't the one?" I realized that I would be doomed to wander through life, searching for her again. I would be on the lookout for her scent, scanning every direction for her smile and dimples. I would tune my ears to the sound of her old soul singing old-school R&B, turning every moment into a song. I would seek out that laugh that's a natural response to her own jokes, even when they're not funny, and that soul that feels like a warm hug, a welcoming home. Realizing this made me decide to propose. Why waste my time searching the world for someone else when the best thing I've ever known has been standing right in front of me all along?

I've always heard people say that love can make you do some crazy things, but I didn't fully grasp that truth until I started planning a proposal. I spent hours scouring YouTube and TikTok videos for inspiration, bouncing ideas off my friends, but nothing seemed quite right. That was until I stumbled upon a social media post that sparked an idea: make a movie! Ahhhhhhh! I knew that was what I was meant to do. As I reflected on all the movies I'd watched over the years, and all the ones we'd watched together, I realized that something was missing from each of them—our story.

So, I decided to make a movie and retell the best love story ever told.

I was stumped in my planning process when I realized that I had to figure out how I was going to get her to watch the movie. *Shoot, I didn't think about that part*, I remember thinking to myself. It just so happened that one of my friends, a photographer, had reached out to see if I wanted to schedule a couple's photoshoot with Netta. I told Netta about this photoshoot but didn't tell her where it would be. On the day of the photoshoot/proposal, I told her that our photographer was renting a space in the Mall of America (this makes sense if you understand how big that mall is—there's literally everything inside; yes, even the egregious thing that you're thinking of). On a snowy April day (yes, you read that correctly), as we made our way through the mall and headed to the theater, she started to get confused. "What are we doing here?" I pretended to be just as confused as she was, making it seem like I was simply following our photographer's instructions.

As we walked into the theater, she saw her parents, who were supposedly out of town for the weekend, and began to cry. At that moment, what we both had been dreaming of was about to come true.

The film began with May 25, 2016, the day we had our first interaction via a Twitter DM (I know, I'm old school). I reenacted all of our key moments: how we had met, how we lost touch and reconnected years later, and how we fell in love with each other. I included some raw footage of the two of us and ended the movie with these lines:

> *If I were to make a movie or write a book about our story, this moment would be the best part—the moment when I ask you to stand in front of our friends and family.*
>
> *The moment when my heart beats and my body begins to feel warm. The moment that I've prayed for and dreamed of.*
>
> *The moment that is even better than how I imagined it in real life.*
>
> *The moment when I get down on one knee and ask you to spend the rest of your life with me.*

As the song "Best Part" played in the background at the end of the movie, I got down on one knee and asked Netta if she would spend the rest of her life with me.

I'm so thankful that God cares about the dreams of little boys, because in just fifteen days, mine will come true, and I will marry my best friend.

PAUSE & REFLECT

What does it feel like to be loved, whether romantically, platonically, or in a familial way? How would you describe it?

Netta and me on June 15, 2024, at A'BULAE in Saint Paul, Minnesota

WHAT'S LOVE GOT TO DO WITH IT?

When I decided to break free and examine the rules of masculinity I was living by, I found that a significant part of my journey was falling in love with love again. In a patriarchal culture, men aren't given the freedom to love without restriction. They are told that their love should be expressed through providing and protecting, and if a straight man shows too much affection—if he writes love letters or speaks with gentleness and kindness—he may be perceived as feminine or gay. In my life, this fear has led me to mask my love, being careful about how I show it to make sure that I could maintain a masculine persona.

I find that our culture, regardless of gender identity or sexual orientation, has a phobia of love. We're so afraid of love that we can barely express it verbally. We're comfortable with quick iterations of it, such as, "Love ya!" or, "Love you, bro," but we rarely utter the phrase, "I love you," as if adding the *I* makes these words too deep and too real. I believe our phobia of love stems from our lack of a clear definition of it: We often see love as a huge, serious thing (not saying it isn't), but love is also the fundamental principle that guides every aspect of our lives.

So, what's love got to do with our lives? Everything. It is embedded in who we are and is what we all need to grow, develop, and survive in this world.

I've never been a dog owner, but I've always been amazed by the difference a dog can make in someone's life—the joy you experience each time you watch your dog wag its tail when it looks at you, or the way it jumps into your arms as if it has waited an entire lifetime to see you again. That's what love is: the profound connection and commitment we feel toward others. As humans, we are wired to form attachments with others or things, which drives our sense of purpose and behavior. Without that attachment or when it's lost, our will to live can easily start to fade away.[18]

Not only does love play a huge role in our survival, but it also drives us to care for the world we live in. We recycle, for instance, because it's a way for us to express our love for the environment and for the future of our children—ensuring that their world won't be filled with waste. Love helps us to reconcile with others when we're in a conflict that feels unresolvable; it's our love for that person or humanity in general that motivates us to seek peace and harmony with others. Love brings life to artistic expression, and also to our faces when it makes us light up, blush, and smile until our cheeks hurt. Love for our community and country compels us to vote responsibly; love makes us curious to learn more about others and step out of our comfort zones.

If I were to define love in my own words, I would borrow from all the definitions I've known of it: the definition found in the Bible, aspects of bell hooks's *All About Love*,[19] Marianne Williamson's *A Return to Love*,[20] and C. S. Lewis's *The Four Loves*.[21] Love is both an action and emotion rooted in a passion and care for something or someone. It is caring—seeking to be kind and affectionate, and acknowledging the physical and emotional needs of humanity. It is

---

18. Alan Eppel, *Sweet Sorrow: Love, Loss and Attachment in Human Life* (London: Routledge, 2018).

19. bell hooks, *All About Love: New Visions* (New York: HarperCollins, 2000).

20. Marianne Williamson, *A Return to Love: Reflections on the Principles of* A Course in Miracles (New York: HarperCollins, 1996).

21. C. S. Lewis, *The Four Loves* (New York: HarperCollins, 1971).

also gracious—seeking to see the heart and beauty of a person and looking beyond a person's flaws or imperfections. It is present—listening, communicating, and being attentive; it mourns with those who mourn and rejoices with those who rejoice. It is respectful—honoring boundaries and treating people the way they want to be treated. It is also vulnerable—requiring us to be open and involving trust. Love is not selfish or envious, nor is it hierarchical or elitist. It is not forced or used as a weapon against someone, and it is never abusive.

In the movie *Get Rich or Die Tryin'*, a drug lord, Majestic, explains the rules of the streets and the drug business to a group of young men in his crew. In my experience, the rules of the streets have always echoed and intersected with the rules of masculinity. The last two rules, I think, speak to masculine perceptions of love. Rule #4: "Don't praise a nigga too much, or else he's gonna think you're soft"; and Rule #5: "Don't show no love, love will get you killed." The phobia of love is rooted in the belief that it makes us soft, which in turn makes us unable to live out the protector role that patriarchy has placed men in.

The danger of patriarchal masculinity is that it cannot coexist with love, as the rules of masculinity are in conflict with the rules of love, which leads many of us to feel shame for showing or receiving it.

Even as I think back to my proposal to Netta, I had to confront my shame. The thoughts that resurfaced from my childhood belief that I was too soft, or the notion that I would be judged for expressing my emotions in such a raw way. But I confronted this shame with love, reminding myself that Netta and I have a mutual and reciprocal love for one another. This is far from shameful—it's actually beautiful.

And if this is what it means to be soft, I hope to be soft for the rest of my life.

PAUSE & REFLECT

If love were a recipe, what would you say are its ingredients?

LOVE, POWER & DOMINANCE

What also gets in the way of our ability to love is our obsession with power and dominance—and I learned this firsthand this past year as I planned our wedding.

I had heard people talking about the process of wedding planning being awful, but nothing could have prepared me for what it would actually be like. First, the cost of weddings is ridiculous, and I can't believe that society normalizes this! Beyond the cost, I think the real battles came with navigating different expectations from both of our families, and the random arguments that arose over picking between this or that. When you're planning a wedding, you're trying to honor the dreams and wishes of many people, and sometimes we all haven't dreamed the same dream. For Netta and me, these differences were things like having an indoor or outdoor wedding, and even something as minor as whether we wanted to remove a certain couch from our venue. I loved the couch and thought it looked great; however, to keep the peace, I yielded to Netta (she absolutely *hated* that couch). The funny thing is that I was yielding to Netta on many things— and I think this was the issue I struggled with the most throughout our planning. What caused me to have a fit was realizing that typical societal patriarchal norms, which are so ingrained in our culture, did not apply to this process.

The most common stereotype about heterosexual weddings is that they are centered around the bride, not the groom. Given this, men are often not in control and are not expected to make the big decisions. When I first got engaged, my boss, Beth, warned me about this. Her advice was to find one or two things that I really cared about and to fight for those things, but to let the other things go. I didn't really believe this would be the case until I noticed the subtle ways in which our venue and even our wedding planner would always defer to what Netta wanted, reminding her that it was her day and ultimately her call. I would sit there, quiet and composed, but internally I was screaming, *What about me? Doesn't my opinion matter? Where is the equality?*[22]

I joke about it now, but seriously, I felt pretty overlooked and powerless in some of those moments.

This feeling made it easy to frame Netta as the villain. I easily constructed a narrative in my mind that Netta wasn't willing to compromise or give up her dream wedding if it conflicted with my ideas. One morning, while processing this, I thought about what I wanted from Netta. The initial thoughts that came up were that I wanted her to take my suggestions and opinions about the wedding seriously. But after a few more sips of coffee, I realized that what I actually wanted was to be in control. I wanted Netta to do what I said, no questions asked, and to adopt all of my suggestions without considering her own desires. In doing so, I was acting in a way that is typical of patriarchal culture—a world that teaches that women, especially those who are romantically involved with men, should do what men want

---

22. Note: When men start talking about how gender equality doesn't apply to them, just know they're likely trolling.

or tell them to do. As I continued to process this while drinking my coffee, I tried to think about what I really cared about—was it really important to me whether we had an indoor or outdoor wedding? Did I really care about this couch?

No, not really.

As I reached the bottom of my coffee mug, I realized that this wasn't about my voice not being heard; it was about power.

What humans often crave about power is the freedom it gives us to pursue our desires and preferences without restriction. A significant portion of our lives is spent striving for it, whether it's seeking promotions at work or accumulating wealth. We work hard to achieve these things because we believe they will allow us to do what we want. Our pursuit of power is typically driven by self-interest rather than a genuine desire to make a positive impact.

The pursuit of power is a fundamental aspect of a patriarchal masculine identity, which emphasizes the dominance and superiority of men in all aspects of life. In this society, men are perceived as better than women and are often ranked above them in various social systems. Many men may appreciate the benefits that women can bring to them (sexually or emotionally, for example), but their desire to maintain their position at the top of the social hierarchy often leads to hatred, resentment, and prejudice against the women and girls they claim to love.

The danger of superiority and hierarchy is that it often leads to violence. It is superiority that motivates genocide. When a culture believes that one group is superior—morally, intellectually, culturally, and physically—they often believe that the world would be better if the other group ceased to exist. Many people may argue that they don't hold this view about women, but we often forget that systems of oppression like White supremacy, patriarchy, and misogyny fly under the radar, floating above us so discreetly that those of us who do not belong to the group experiencing oppression will never hear its loud sound or see the large aircraft. While many of us will never say the words, "I hate women," we show it through the sexist language we use and the harassment we allow women and girls to undergo, treating it like it's just a rite of passage. We show we hate women by shaming them for their natural bodily appearance, such as having hair on their body, or for putting on too much makeup; we also show we hate women in the many ways that we subtly assume they cannot be leaders.

I remember when I first started one of my jobs as a diversity, equity, and inclusion trainer. During my first week, I shadowed a workshop facilitated by two colleagues who were women, and one of them held a PhD. I had no idea what I was doing or what was happening, yet every time someone entered the room before the training started, they would bypass my women colleagues and approach me directly. They would then ask me for guidance, only for me to refer them back to my colleagues who had been ignored, clearly indicating that they believed I was the most knowledgeable and capable of helping them. These incidents of everyday sexism and microaggressions eventually create the pathway for violence against women and girls. A woman may be ignored once and then called a demeaning word in the next moment. When a society believes that a particular group is inferior, they become comfortable with the dehumanization and injustice that this group faces.

To put the picture together, if power and dominance are rooted in individual self-interest and control over others, can love coexist with it? Can men truly love themselves and others if they believe their masculinity is rooted in patriarchy, a system that perpetuates men's superiority and that is based on the oppression of women, girls, and other gender minorities?

Grappling with these questions and coming to the conclusion that they cannot is what makes this work so pivotal. Love and oppression cannot coexist with each other.

RESPONDING TO PRIVILEGE WITH LOVE

Although we as men are harmed by the patriarchy as I've uncovered throughout this book, it's also important to recognize that we still benefit from it greatly. Because of that, it is our responsibility to use our collective power to resist this harmful system. Resisting the patriarchy is one of the greatest acts of love we can perform in our lifetime.

The reality about privilege—which is the unearned access to power based on our social identities—is that we don't have a choice about whether we have it or not. Because of this, we are left with the question of what we should do about the privilege we yield. We can get defensive about this privilege and try to deny its existence—I've often seen men do this by citing rising male suicide rates, using the statistic as a way to discredit the privilege that men have. A key fact about male privilege of any kind is that it does not mean that your life is not hard, nor does it mean that bad things don't happen to you. Rather, it means that your identity or your maleness is not systemically making your life harder. Though patriarchy harms us all, we need to look at who it harms and impacts the most, and who it grants power to. Our response to this privilege can manifest as guilt, and we may sit with these guilty feelings for having privilege. However, guilt may not lead us to take action. Overall, I argue that our response to our privilege should be love—and loving means investing in taking the system down that oppresses others.

As an anti-racism trainer, I often receive questions from White participants about how to get involved and continue working toward advancing racial justice. The challenge lies in providing a response that acknowledges the unique journey of each individual, as there is no one-size-fits-all approach to fighting for justice. Rather than conforming to a specific method or feeling pressured to follow someone else's lead, I encourage my White participants to leverage their unique gifts, talents, and spheres of influence to challenge inequity and amplify the voices of Black, Brown, and Indigenous individuals.

Similarly, I urge men to take an active role in fighting against patriarchy by living out their authentic masculinity in whole and healthy ways. This can involve using their talents and skills to make a positive impact. For example, writers can blog about their experiences of unlearning patriarchal masculinity, while coaches can incorporate lessons on healthy masculinity into their coaching styles. Leaders can conduct equity audits, examine their pay scales, and ensure that their leadership teams are diverse and inclusive. Perhaps most importantly, men can start having conversations with other men about these issues, as men are often more likely to be receptive to hearing these messages from fellow men.

The key is to find an authentic way to get involved and take action. By doing so, we can collectively create a powerful movement that is centered on loving all of humanity regardless of race, class, ability, sexuality, or gender.

PAUSE & REFLECT

What are some ways you can leverage your power
and privilege to challenge and dismantle patriarchal
masculinity?

DEVOTIONAL

What's interesting about society's perception of Jesus is that I think it can sometimes be one-sided. Yes, we all know that Jesus was from a lower social class and was unhoused; we know that he was arrested on some bogus charges and sentenced to death by the Roman government. While we know that Jesus was a man who experienced oppression and marginalization, he was also a man who held power. He was a male, born in a patriarchal culture and society, and was also seen as a rabbi—a wise and religious teacher who preached sermons and interpreted scriptures. In the Christian faith, we also believe that Jesus is the Son of God, therefore he is also divine. In his divinity, he performed miraculous things—he turned water into wine, made food multiply, cast out demons, and healed those who were sick. As you can imagine, if Jesus lived today, there would be videos of his miracles going viral on social media. The news would constantly be reporting on and following Jesus's ministry, trying to capture what he would do next. Although in Jesus's time they didn't have the same methods we have to spread information, they spread the word nonetheless. Crowds often followed Jesus, and everyone was trying to figure out what was the mystery of this man.

What I love about Jesus and what I think we can all learn from him is how he utilized his power. Although Jesus had ample opportunities to capitalize and profit off his supernatural abilities, he could have (if he wanted to) used his positional and social capital to get whatever he wanted, whenever he wanted. Instead, he chose to live a simple life—he wore plain clothing, traveled on foot, and didn't seek recognition from crowds. This is in stark contrast to how many big leaders of the church live today—megachurch leaders who are known for their flashy lifestyles and exorbitant speaking fees. In the world of social media influencers and a capitalist society, we are often consumed by our desire to make more money and increase our power.

Yet, Jesus—Messiah, teacher, healer, savior—used his power to love humanity.

An example of this is found in Jesus's journey to Galilee, where he arrived at a Samaritan town and encountered a Samaritan woman drawing water from a well alone. It's worth noting that it was unusual for women to draw water from wells alone during that time. This was often a social activity, similar to modern-day barbershops or salons, where people would gather to build community and gossip about local happenings. This raises a question: Why was this woman alone?

Jesus asked the woman for a drink, a request that initially surprised and unsettled the woman due to the societal stigmas and norms of the time—a Jewish man engaging with a Samaritan woman was considered highly irregular and perhaps even frowned upon. Her response, "How is it that thou, being a Jew, askest drink of me, who am a Samaritan woman?" (John 4:9, ASV), reveals the social barriers and prejudices that existed between their communities.

This moment highlights another characteristic of Jesus: He pushes beyond social barriers. A key thing to know about Jewish and Samaritan people is that both groups couldn't reconcile their differences. They didn't agree on how to worship, how to interpret scriptures, or what it meant to truly honor God. Because of this, they existed in total separation, which often manifested as pure hatred for one another. I find that the political world of today has a similar dynamic as Jewish- and Samaritan-like groups—democrat, republican, liberal, and conservative. Although these two political outlooks have some differences that may never be reconciled, I'm always reminded by Jesus that our disdain or frustration with those we've deemed as "the other side" does not diminish their humanity—it does not make them undeserving of love. Simply by approaching this woman, Jesus was breaking the rules that his culture lived by.

As the story unfolds, Jesus offered the woman living water, symbolizing spiritual truth and eternal satisfaction. Intrigued by this offer, the woman requested this water, and here is where the story becomes beautifully messy.

Jesus asked her to go and call her husband and then return. She responded that she didn't have one. Then Jesus revealed that he knew that she had multiple husbands and was currently living with a man who was not her husband. In this moment, we gain insight into why the woman was alone at the well in the first place—the community knew her situation, and they probably avoided being seen with her or talking to her so they wouldn't be shamed. No one wanted to be friends with "that girl."

And yet, Jesus, already knowing the truth about her background, still came to her and asked for a drink from the well. This could have been a perfect time for him to tell the woman about the wrong she was doing in her life; he could have pulled out his rabbi card and started throwing Old Testament scriptures at her (this was probably how many people would have wanted and expected him to respond). But instead, he simply asked her for a drink of water. When Jesus brought up her husband, he was acknowledging that he saw her truth—although he already knew about her situation, he still approached her. This interaction changed the woman's life, and she went on to tell everyone what Jesus did for her.

While it was undoubtedly Jesus's divinity that changed her life, I draw parallels and nuggets from this story about what love and truly seeing someone can do. I also reflect on how we can use our social power to uplift others rather than ourselves.

Perhaps this is the beauty of love: When we put it into action, it will compel us to move beyond barriers and differences. Through my experiences in churches of various denominations, cultures, and traditions, I've observed that the church has a complex and often contradictory relationship with love. On one hand, love is deeply embedded in our faith—it's impossible to discuss Christianity without discussing love, as seen in the command to "love your neighbor as you love yourself" (the second greatest commandment according to Jesus). On the other hand, I believe that the church is afraid of love, and perhaps this is why we often struggle to mention love without adding a caveat such as the phrase, "Love the sinner, hate the sin." This dichotomy highlights the tension between our professed values of love and our actual actions.

The issue with this saying is that it creates an "us vs. them" culture and reinforces a hierarchy by assigning labels to people. In other words, we love the idea of a "sinner" because we don't see ourselves as one but rather view it as a label applied to "those people over there." This separation and assigning of labels lead to a toxic habit of diminishing people's humanity, which is not how God interacts with us. God knows the labels we might deserve, God knows the labels that society gives us, but instead God chooses to call us by our names.

Jesus never said, "Love the sinner, hate the sin." Instead, he simply commanded us to love our neighbor. This command sounds inspiring, but it's much harder to put into practice. In many ways, we've watered down and reduced love to merely being "nice" or saying hello when we pass someone on the street.

Love requires us to go deeper than that. It requires us to be like Jesus in this story—not using our power as a tool of oppression but rather as an agent for liberation.

Our love can be liberating when it humanizes others—especially those with whom we disagree. When I encounter someone who holds opinions different from mine, I try my best to learn their stories and lived experiences that have shaped them. Even if I can't humanize their opinion, I can humanize the stories and better understand why a person thinks the way they think. I call this loving curiosity. With loving curiosity, our first goal when encountering tension or disagreement is to put aside the desire to prove that we're right or the desire to judge or condemn, and simply try to understand and meet that person where they are.

PAUSE & REFLECT

What rules might we need to break to love our neighbor better?

X

WHOLENESS

"Authenticity, to me, is the unwavering commitment to being true to oneself, even in the face of societal constructs.

Yet, masculinity, with its rigid definitions and constraints, can sometimes hinder the journey toward authenticity, obscuring the path with expectations and demands. This challenges us to navigate this maze by always being honest with ourselves and staying true to who we are."

DEMETRIUS CHESTER, GOLDEN VALLEY, MN

"BE WHO YOU SAY YOU ARE"

Eric Walker and I met in 2016 at Folwell Hall on the University of Minnesota campus, where we both attended an interest meeting for Phi Beta Sigma Fraternity, Inc. I knew that I wanted to pledge in the fall, and this meeting was a chance for me to scope out my potential line brothers. In the world of Black Greekdom, your line brothers are the group of men who join the fraternity with you and are the people you're usually closest to in the organization. As I got to know Eric at the meeting, I kept thinking to myself: *I hope I don't pledge with him.* Eric reminded me a lot of my older brother, with whom I had a lot of tension until my adult life. He was a Division 1 track star, accustomed to receiving attention from a lot of women, and was known for being a smooth and slick talker— able to talk his way out of any situation and always eager to remind others that he was from "the strong side," the South Side of Chicago.

He fit the masculine archetype of what a "cool" guy would be, and in many ways, Eric had what a lot of men wanted. He was a fearless individual, not really afraid of anyone or anything, and if you ever started a fight with him, he wouldn't hesitate to finish it. He was a straight shooter, always transparent and authentic. With him, you knew exactly what you were getting. He was the kind of person who wouldn't compromise his identity for anyone—he wouldn't hesitate to wear a durag with a suit to a professional event and would never let anyone dictate how he expressed himself.

For better or for worse, he would say what he wanted, do what he wanted, and wouldn't apologize for it.

After joining the fraternity together with two other men, Eric and I developed a relationship that was similar to most of my relationships with men—a mix of closeness and distance. Although I was only a few months older than Eric, he was like a big brother to me. I always felt physically safe in his presence, and I followed him wherever he led me. Eric was probably one of the only people who could convince me to attend a party with him. I was known for being the introvert who was always "inside," but one call from Eric and all of a sudden I was on my way to the place I had just told all of our friends

I wasn't going to. We may not have been close in the "talk every day" kind of way—we could go some long periods of time without seeing each other. Nonetheless, we both knew that we had each other's back if and when we ever needed each other.

On September 3, 2022, Eric was killed in a car accident.

I struggled to process his death because I couldn't shake off my feelings of guilt. The distance that existed between Eric and me was a result of my own insecurity. He was constantly inviting me into his life, suggesting we hang out, and even throwing mini birthday dinners for me almost every year during the six years we knew each other. Despite his constant invitations to spend time together, I consistently declined, afraid to be vulnerable and to get to know him better. I was scared that he would discover the truth—that I wasn't like him, and that if he knew that, he would no longer want to be my brother.

The power of shame lies in its ability to make us self-select our rejection, allowing us to avoid the possibility of it. In other words, I created a narrative that dictated how I interacted with other men, one in which Eric and others like him would never accept me for who I was. As I let this narrative shape my actions and relationships, I ensured that it was never challenged.

Eric and I were distant because I had never given him the chance to get close.

After Eric's passing, a picture of the mirror in his apartment was posted on social media, with the phrase, "Be who you say you are," written directly on the glass surface—his mantra. This phrase became a refrain in my mind, echoing repeatedly after his death. This was the rule that Eric lived by, and I felt deeply convicted by it. At the time, I was largely defined by who I was around, and I knew how to adapt my performance to suit the audience, but these different roles often conflicted with each other since their values and opinions clashed. And when the curtain call came on each of those performances, I would leave feeling empty.

Because of my own guilt and tension, I never had the opportunity to say anything about Eric at the memorial event (Omega Ceremony) our fraternity held for him. I kept thinking, *I shouldn't be the one to say anything; other people knew him better.* I regret it deeply. If I could go back in time, I would start by telling those gathered that I was first in line, known as the "ace," and Eric was second, or "deuce." During New Member Presentations, when we would reveal to campus that we had joined the fraternity, many people assumed that the ace, being placed in the front, is the leader. However, Eric was the true leader of our line, and it was an honor to always have him behind me. From his position, he could see what I couldn't, and he was perfectly positioned to push me forward.

I'm not sure if Eric ever knew how much I needed those pushes. While he was alive, Eric pushed me to explore, venture beyond my comfort zone, and even in his death he pushed me to stop being afraid of letting the world know who I am.

I now try to bring my authentic self to every space I enter, reminding myself that I can never truly experience acceptance or rejection unless I'm willing to be seen. While I can't say that I do this perfectly, I've made progress in leaving behind the need to conform to others' expectations. I still find myself thinking about Eric and the way he lived life unapologetically, and that influence is the legacy he left with me.

Although Eric's life may have been cut short, his words, his mantra, and his existence in my life has forever changed who I am.

In Loving Memory of Eric Walker (April 1, 1997 – September 3, 2022). This photo captures the two of us at the Minnesota NPHC Greek Picnic on August 19, 2021, where Eric (on the right) as always, brought so much joy, laughter, and love to us all.

PAUSE & REFLECT

Who do you say you are, and how do you live it out?
Are there any inconsistencies, and if so, when do you
notice them?

CODE-SWITCHING

To *be* who we are, we need to first *know* who we are. What makes
knowing ourselves and embodying our truth so challenging is the
code-switching that society demands of us based on our identities.
We often learn how to code-switch through cultural osmosis, rather
than explicit instruction. For example, in the United States, Whiteness and White culture are the dominant standards, and regardless
of one's racial background, society will constantly ask us to assimilate to these norms. This forced assimilation is evident in schools
and workplaces, where we see restrictions on Black hairstyles, such
as policies against braids or locs, or restrictions on playing certain
music genres like hip-hop/rap. Additionally, language is also restricted,
with students being told they can only speak "proper English" and
not other dialects.

What a world built on White supremacy does is demonize Black
culture, and it calls any and everything associated with Blackness
"bad" (or in the workplace "unprofessional"). In this world, to be who
you are is not acceptable; therefore, to move up the social ladder, or
sometimes just to be safe, we change our hair, change the way we talk
and dress, and temporarily become who they want us to be until we
are able to return to the communities that allow us to be who we are.

Similar to code-switching based on race and cultural identity, I think men also have to code-switch to follow dominant-culture masculinity. When a world is built on patriarchy, it expects dominance and superiority from its men, as we have learned, meaning that men will feel a societal pressure to assimilate to patriarchal masculinity. As a result, men are often forced to perform a certain way even when there are aspects of themselves that don't align with a patriarchal model. These aspects aren't always cut off or removed but are sometimes placed into different compartments of their lives. This is why men often engage in the practice of compartmentalization—placing their interests, thoughts, and emotions into different sections. For example, if society judges men by their ability to handle challenges independently, persevere in adversity, and maintain a stoic demeanor, then a man must compartmentalize his emotions and vulnerabilities once he steps into the public eye.

For some men, this entails going to work and pretending to be emotionally well even when facing distress in their personal lives. He convinces himself that at work, he is composed, free from life's struggles, and everything is fine. He asserts his strength. This type of compartmentalizing is often how men avoid pain. Instead of grieving a loss or processing a heartache, emotions that they do not want to experience get tucked away and are never fully processed. This is why, for some, when a person they were extremely close to passes away, they may find themselves suddenly grieving all the other losses they had failed to process years or even decades ago. This is because their current grief has opened up that compartment where the memories of other losses were stored.

In patriarchal societies, real men are seen as soldiers—those who fight in wars. What defines these soldiers as real men is their ability to set aside their emotions, and sometimes even their morals and values, for the so-called "greater good." These men may participate directly or indirectly in the killing of innocent civilians and children, justifying their actions based on the compartment they occupy as a soldier, separate from their civilian life. Men who frequently engage in the practice of compartmentalizing rarely bring their fullest self to any space they enter. They have versions of who they are, and these versions sometimes have different values and beliefs, often leading to cognitive dissonance.

I experienced an element of this dissonance when I first transferred from my private Christian school to a public school in fourth grade. Upon my arrival at J.J. Hill Montessori School, I didn't play with the other boys at first during recess. You could find me playing tetherball with the girls or playing hand games like "slide-slide-slippery-slide" somewhere else on the playground. This worked well in the beginning, until I learned that this wasn't how boys were supposed to play. As I learned more and more about the social rules of elementary school, I slowly started to shift—replacing my tetherball with a football, and my hand games with card games. *This was the normal way to be*, I thought to myself. Every year in school after fourth grade, I felt like I had to decide who I would be that year. As I got to junior high, the distance between masculinity and femininity became clearer, and I had to ask myself whether I would be myself or whether I would "man up." I decided that I would do both—being one of the guys when I was with them, and someone else when I wasn't around them.

This became the recipe for how I lived my life going forward, a recipe that would never produce wholeness but would instead strip me of it. One of my friends, who is still my friend to this day, tried to help me realize this during my junior year of college when she staged an intervention or reality check with me. "I don't know, D," she said to me in my campus apartment. "I think you've just changed, and I'm not the only one who's noticed." In this moment, she was bringing awareness to the fact that these worlds were bleeding together and impacting each other. It was like a moment from those special Disney Channel episodes where characters from one show would be featured on another, and we as viewers know the irony—the characters exist in a different world yet seem oblivious to it. Initially, I responded to this reality check with defensiveness. *She doesn't even know me like that*, I thought to myself, wanting to ignore the ways in which I was lacking integrity.

It wasn't until years later that I realized she was right.

As I reflected on our conversation, I became aware of how my life, which had once been void of men, was now full of them after joining a fraternity—and I wanted to have the best of both worlds. I wanted to be myself with my women friends, and I wanted to be able to be one of the guys, too. My platonic relationships with women have probably played the largest role in developing me into who I am. Through their stories, I learned about the challenges women face and saw directly how the men in their lives treated and interacted with them. And when I first joined the fraternity, I became a part of the group of men that my women friends always talked about. The ones who hurt them and often made them cry. With my fraternity brothers, I would laugh at things that I never would have laughed at around my women friends. I wouldn't blink an eye anytime someone said something misogynistic or homophobic, and I actively engaged in derogatory chants and strolls.[23]

In one world, I was considered the "safest" man whom many women knew, and in another, I laughed and participated in the things that made their world unsafe.

PAUSE & REFLECT

Has your performance of masculinity ever impacted your ability to maintain your integrity? If so, how?

BECOMING WHO WE ARE

Throughout this book, I've taken you on a personal journey, sharing with you various stories from my upbringing and childhood that have shaped my understanding of masculinity and informed the ways I've lived my life. I didn't write this book to tell you who you should be, but rather to examine the rules we live by and to expose how these rules may be hiding our true selves. A question that I think we should all ask ourselves is this: Who would we be if the existence of shame ceased? If, in a utopian world, no one cared about what you wore, how you looked, or what your interests were, what music would you dance to, what colors would you like, and what would you do for fun?

---

23. Strolling is a tradition within Black Greek-letter organizations, also known as the Divine Nine. This tradition is a dance that is done in a vertical line, typically involving stepping and modern dance moves, and often accompanied by chants related to one's organization. Each organization has multiple "strolls," and for fraternities, some of these may include making sexually suggestive gestures with the hands or body, as well as corresponding chants with explicit language.

Our response to this question likely reveals who we would be when we are our most authentic and whole selves.

Many of the issues I face in my life, including social anxiety, depression, and compulsive shopping, are all connected to my inability to be whole and to live with integrity. When I live by the rules of masculinity, I lead a life that is inconsistent with who I am. In that life, I'm constantly asked to perform, and like most people, when we perform in front of crowds, we get nervous—we worry about saying our lines right, maintaining the proper tone, and using the correct body language. The anxiety-inducing nature of a patriarchal masculine performance is that it rarely ends; therefore, the assessment never does. What's most devastating to our sense of self and our mental health is when the role assigned to us by patriarchy conflicts with our values. At the foundation of who we are is our values, and when we live outside of them, we live outside of who we are. When we stray from our true selves, we lose our sense of purpose, the feeling that gives our lives meaning and direction.

When we live in opposition to our values, we can't be well.

When I was twelve or thirteen years old, I contemplated taking my life. What I remember most about this contemplation was a feeling of hopelessness—I felt I had lost my sense of purpose, and that there was no reason for me to continue living. I thought that maybe the world would be better off without me. Years later, when these same thoughts and contemplations resurfaced, I realized that they were connected to the endless pressure of trying to be what everyone wanted me to be, rather than being who I am.

The question then becomes: how do we become who we are? My response to this question is both simple and complicated.

We become who we are by trusting that we know who we are.

In my journey of self-discovery, I read countless self-help books, which were helpful, but they couldn't provide a definitive answer to this question. I searched for answers in books, changes in my appearance, and shifting interests, hoping to find language that would describe who I am. What I had to come to realize was that I've always known who I am—I've known what I like and dislike, I am aware of the culture in which I was raised, and I have dreams that propel me toward my future. What I needed to do was trust the voice that sang relentlessly in the shower, the boy who danced fiercely when no one was watching, and the adult who still gets lost in their imagination today. It's not that I never knew who I was; I just didn't believe it. Instead, I allowed the expectations and rules from patriarchy and society to shape my identity.

A great first step in building trust with yourself is to return to the memories of your childhood. There's something authentic about children, who are brutally honest and uninhibited. They don't hesitate to express their likes and dislikes, and in their innocence, they are free from societal pressures. When we explore our childhood identity, we can look for echoes of our current life. For instance, I'm a huge pacer. I spend a lot of time pacing around my home, and I don't think it's a result of anxiety as much as it is a remnant of my childhood love of dancing and moving my body. When societal expectations shamed me for dancing, pacing became a discreet way to express myself without being judged. By continuing to trust ourselves, we allow ourselves to speak our truth, saying or writing what we think, and stopping the self-silencing that occurs when we try to conform to others' expectations. We trust ourselves when we listen to the whispers of our body and attend to the clues it gives us about our emotions.

When we do this, we follow the mantra of Eric Walker and truly become who we say we are.

DEVOTIONAL

What I've found to be the most difficult thing about getting to a place of wholeness and having the courage to be myself is healing from the things that have suppressed or blocked my awareness of who I am.

Our life is full of many things that have stripped us of this awareness: the messages that others have told us, which have led to shame or to believing that we are not good enough, smart enough, or man enough; the traumas that we've faced in our lives that have altered our perceptions of ourselves or the world; and the rules of masculinity that we live by, which tell us to be something or someone that we're not. In order for us to be whole, we must deal with and heal from these things. However, as I'm sure many of you already know, healing is no easy journey.

The difficult part about healing is that it looks different in everyone's life. While we can glean nuggets of wisdom from the stories and experiences of others, ultimately, what aided me on my journey may not be the same for you, and the places where I needed to stop to address "unfinished business" may differ from yours. In other words, there is no magic recipe for healing. There is no book or resource that will outline your journey perfectly for you. Healing is not that straightforward; it's not a linear process that unfolds like a ladder against a wall. Rather, it's a messy course with ups and downs, curves and twists.

The Bible is full of many stories of healing, and my favorite is found in Matthew 9:20–21. This story is about a very brave and courageous woman who suffered with a blood issue for twelve very long years. When Luke recounts this story, he mentions that the woman had tried various methods of healing and had seen various doctors, but no one could fix it. It is likely that this woman had heard about Jesus's ability to heal the sick and raise the dead, and when she saw him, she saw hope. This hope led her to take a risk, and she touched the hem of Jesus's garment, saying to herself that if she could just touch it, she would be made whole (Matthew 9:21). The woman who suffered for twelve years was healed instantly. When Jesus realized that power had left his body, he turned around, saw the woman, and called her "daughter" (KJV). He told her that her faith had made her whole.

The unwritten part of the story is the immense courage it took for this woman to do what she did. In the ancient world, and even in our world today, we often see people with sickness or disease as dirty or unclean, and we treat them as if they are less than. We assign labels to them, just as they did to this woman. Thousands of years later as we read her story, we still don't know her by name and only know her by her condition. When we define people by their issues, we minimize their humanity—we reduce them to being addicted, unhoused, abused, or incarcerated, which reflects their circumstances, not their identity. The stigma surrounding the woman's bleeding likely isolated her from everyone in her community. People didn't want to be around those who were labeled "unclean." Yet Jesus looked at her and rebranded her as a daughter—one who is loved and protected, and who belongs to someone.

While not all of us may have a blood issue that marginalizes us, we all have something that hinders our wholeness, and we all have struggles with issues that we've faced for many years.

One of the issues I struggled with was the secret of my molestation. The shame and stigma that accompanied it brought me down, until I grew tired of hiding. And just like the woman in that story who sought out many things to fix herself, in the same way I sought out awards and achievements, believing that doing great things would make me forget the bad things. My healing actually came from the decision to start telling the truth. A concept so simple, yet so hard in practice—just like touching Jesus's garment appears to be a simple gesture, but when you know all that the woman had to go through, you can see that this was no easy act of faith.

Wholeness begins with the truth. The challenge that exists within many churches and places of worship is the culture of shame, which creates an environment that supports lies to cover things up more than it supports truth-telling. Of course, this doesn't apply to all churches, but far too often these places where we claim the broken can be made whole are places where the broken become further fragmented. Sometimes we amplify the flaws or brokenness in others, believing that it makes us more whole. We all struggle in some way, and these struggles may look different for each person, but we're called to give others the same grace that we so quickly give to ourselves.

The woman had to be honest with herself about her condition in order to muster up the faith to touch Jesus. The response that Jesus gives her also teaches us an important lesson. Jesus's telling her that it was her faith that made her whole reminds us that our wholeness and healing is our own responsibility. We may not have caused the pain or trauma, or created the rule book that fragmented our lives, but deciding to take the course of healing is our responsibility. No one can force you to address the stories in your life that echo into your present—that is entirely on you.

And the beauty of this is that when we tell our own stories, we get to control how they are told. We get to determine what details we share with others, and what parts we leave for ourselves to uncover. We get to resist the oppressive systems that seek to erase, rewrite, or silence our stories, and we get to prioritize our own healing through the authentic and honest testimony of our experiences.

For my own journey of healing and wholeness, I had to unlearn patriarchal masculinity, which was like my own blood issue that I had suffered with for many years. My pursuit of healing consisted of a lot of prayer, and a lot of silence. It was a process that involved reading and reflecting, crying and writing; sometimes it looked like empty bottles of wine, and sometimes consisted of emptying myself spiritually. Your journey may include none of these things or all of them, but what's most important is that you take these steps forward, regardless of what they look like.

Writing this book has been a step along the way in my journey to healing. As I shared each story in these pages, some of which I've told many times and others that I've never told before, I allowed my words to set me free. With each page, I uncovered what was hiding behind the mask that patriarchy told me to wear, and just like the nine-year-old boy that Tony Porter described in his TED Talk:

Without that mask, I am free.

PAUSE & REFLECT

The woman said to herself that if she could just touch the hem of Jesus's garment, she would be made whole. I ask you: what might you need to touch, to revisit, to process, or to heal from so that you, too, can be made whole?

EPILOGUE

A tradition of my podcast and social media content is to conclude each post or podcast episode with a letter written to men. These letters are not a random marketing tool or creative gesture—no. There's a story behind them.

Several years ago, I was experiencing a depressive episode, and I found myself caught in a cycle of shame. Past mistakes came to the surface, and I didn't know what to do with them. I desperately craved affirmation, seeking a voice that would echo through the silence and reach my ears. I longed for a secret letter in the mail addressed to me, telling me that someone loved me, that I wasn't a doomed mistake, and that my imperfections and errors didn't make me unlovable. I was looking for some sort of miraculous encounter with God that would change everything, but instead, I remember hearing a lot of silence—despite the noise surrounding me. I expressed this feeling to one of my therapist, who responded by asking me, "What if you wrote this letter to yourself?" This led to a practice in our therapy sessions: learning to trust my own voice. When I needed affirmation or advice, she would ask me to pause, and instead of asking her for it, she would tell me to close my eyes and ask myself what I needed. I would respond out loud, and she would say, "That's what you needed." While affirmation from outside sources is still valid and important, there are also moments where the encouragement we desperately need and desire comes from within.

Looking back on those nights when I waited patiently for God to speak to me, I've come to realize that God was waiting for me to trust and believe in what had already been spoken over my life since I was a child.

As this book comes to a close, I want to conclude with a personal letter written to myself, and then I'm putting the ball in your court— take the next few pages to write a letter to yourself. As you've uncovered how we're shamed for not fitting into societal boxes based on how "man enough" we are or how our physical bodies look, what do you need to tell yourself? As you've uncovered how patriarchal masculinity strips us of our softness and gentleness and only allows us to be angry, what does that stir up for you? Whether it's how we've navigated silence and accountability, brotherhood and fatherhood, love or wholeness, what affirmation do you most need in this moment?

I'll go first.

July 2, 2024

Dear Destyn,

We've been on this journey together for quite some time now. As you're writing this book and feeling anxious about the possibilities of its reception—whether it will reach anyone, if it will languish on a shelf forever, or if no one will even read it—I want you to remember that I'm so proud of you for writing it anyway. As you feel worried about what people may think about you based on your stories, or if they will question your faith or other aspects of who you are, remember that one of the most courageous things you can do is to tell the truth.

I remember the composition notebook you wrote in when you were nine years old—in that notebook, you told the secrets of being molested. You covered the notebook in tape and wrote the words, "Keep out!" all over it (by the way, that wasn't very discreet at all). In your early adulthood, you stripped your room and searched your parents' basement to find this notebook, hoping to get to it before they did. You looked for this notebook because you thought you needed it to "prove" what happened, what actually happened, or to believe that what you'd already known was true. Eventually, you gave up searching for it and decided to rewrite it—and this time not to keep it hidden but to free yourself and others, too.

Speaking of hiding—don't forget that you have a light that brightens every room you enter, so don't hide it! Smile until your cheeks ache, laugh until it cramps your stomach, sing until your voice grows tired, and dance until your feet are sore. Your joy is too contagious to be confined; it's meant to be shared with others. And your light is too brilliant to be hidden under a bushel. As Marianne

Williamson so wisely said, don't ask yourself, "Who am I to be brilliant, gorgeous, talented, fabulous?" Go and tell yourself, "Actually, who are you not to be?"[24]

Your journey has largely consisted of you trying to prove yourself to the world. You've accomplished many impressive things throughout your life, and in this chapter of life, you feel surrounded by love and acceptance. Don't forget—the love and acceptance you feel is not based on what you've accomplished; it's wrapped up in who you are. It's your silliness, which always tells jokes and makes awkward moments feel normal; your gentle heart that can have small talk with a stranger for as long as they need; and your words that make people feel like they can always feel comforted—this is why you're loved. You're loved for your wisdom and advice that goes beyond your years, and for the courage you show every time you tell your story. You're also loved simply for existing. It doesn't matter who you will become or what you will look like—your parents, family, and many others still love you.

When insecurity arises, whether it's about the way your body looks, how you compare to others in your life, or if you're following everyone's expectations of you, remember that you are and have always been enough. Meaning you don't have to try to be "man enough," strong enough, tough enough, or whatever you choose to fill in

---

24. Marianne Williamson, *A Return to Love: Reflections on the Principles of* A Course in Miracles (New York: HarperCollins, 1996).

the blanks. As your neighbor James has told you since you were a young boy, you are Destyn (*destined*) for greatness.

You are loved and accepted, and don't forget—this is just one part of your story; there's so much more even after this.

Until the next chapter,
Destyn Land

I now invite you to do the same.

ACKNOWLEDGMENTS

Special thanks to:

Dr. Jeremy Myers, whose 2018 class provided the foundation for my involvement in this project. The final paper I wrote in your class has grown into the book you now hold. Thank you for your guidance, mentorship, and friendship.

The Polaris fellowship at Princeton Theological Seminary, which offered me the support and resources necessary to turn my dreams into reality. This book was written as a project for the fellowship. I would like to extend my gratitude to Azucena "Ceni" De La Torre and Shari Oosting for affirming my vision and walking alongside me on this journey. I am also grateful to the rest of the inaugural Polaris cohort, who served as cheerleaders, thought partners, and friends to lean on throughout my writing process.

Demetrius Chester, who has been a constant source of spiritual guidance and wisdom throughout my writing journey. I often found myself feeling insecure about what the Church would think about what I've written, and you were always there to assure me that this work I'm doing is indeed the work of the Lord. Thank you for being a trusted friend and brother.

Kimberley Lim, whose editorial assessment and copy edit have truly made this book what it is today. Words cannot express how grateful I am for her critical eye, which pushed me to go deeper and expand my ideas. Your collaboration brought so much life and enjoyment to this book. Thank you for your affirmation, and for being willing to take on this project.

To my friends and family, who have encouraged me to pursue my dreams with passion and purpose. And I am especially grateful for my wife, Richnetta—I love you.

AUTHOR'S BIO

Born and raised in the historically Black Rondo community of St. Paul, Minnesota, Destyn's upbringing instilled in him a deep appreciation for his roots and a strong sense of community. From a young age, Destyn showcased musical abilities, demonstrating exceptional talent as a piano player. Simultaneously, Destyn discovered a passion for writing, likely inherited from his father who has written two books. This ability allowed him to articulate his thoughts and explore his unique perspective on masculinity during a final paper for an undergraduate Youth Studies class. It was in this class that Destyn saw the issue with patriarchal masculinity.

Inspired by this revelation, Destyn pursued further education, completing a Master of Education in Youth Development Leadership in 2021 from the University of Minnesota Twin Cities and a Bachelor of Arts in English Literature, Language, and Theory in 2019 from Augsburg University in Minneapolis, Minnesota. His academic journey led him to delve into the construction of Black masculinity and conduct research on how it influences young Black boys. This formed the foundation for his ongoing mission to promote healthy masculinity and challenge the harmful effects of patriarchal structures.

In 2022, Destyn launched the podcast and Instagram account *Rethinking Manhood*, amassing over four thousand followers and attracting listeners from 57 different countries and 605 cities. Through this platform, Destyn fearlessly confronts the impact of patriarchy on men, encouraging transformative discussions and advocating for positive change.

In the following year, Destyn was selected to be a part of the inaugural group of Princeton Theological Seminary's Polaris fellowship. Leveraging his gift for writing and storytelling, Destyn developed *The Rules We Live By*, a book that guides men and individuals exploring masculinity toward understanding the harm imposed by patriarchal ideals. Through thoughtful reflections and engaging activities, he aims to pave the way for a healthier and more inclusive expression of masculinity.

To learn more about Destyn and his work, visit

DESTYNLAND.COM

Made in the USA
Monee, IL
16 November 2024